YOU CAN'T FIX WHAT
YOU CAN'T SEE

YOU CAN'T FIX WHAT YOU CAN'T SEE

AN EYE-OPENING TOOLKIT FOR CULTIVATING GENDER HARMONY IN BUSINESS

KAREN F. CORNWELL

NEW DEGREE PRESS

YOU CAN'T FIX WHAT YOU CAN'T SEE

An Eye-Opening Toolkit for Cultivating Gender Harmony in Business

ISBN   978-1-64137-341-8   *Paperback*

         978-1-64137-662-4   *Ebook*

To My Three Sons:

Zachary

Joshua & Skylar

May Your World be a Better Place!

CONTENTS

Never doubt that a small group of thoughtful, committed people can change the world. Indeed, it is the only thing that ever has.

– MARGARET MEAD

INTRODUCTION

―――

Your purpose in life is to find your purpose and give your whole heart and soul to it.

—BUDDHA

"I don't see the problem you are trying to solve."

I was growing confused. *How can he not see it?*

You DON'T see the problem? I was still shaking my head from side to side, as if trying to clear the fog. *How could this be true? It's unfathomable to me. I was expecting to get a lot of great feedback from Dale, but not this! It's like slamming into a brick wall as soon as you leave the starting gate.*

I thought I knew him. I respected him. I had worked for him. I had even hired him as a consultant at another company.

I was losing faith. If he couldn't see it, how could he help me? After all, you can't fix what you can't see.

***

Less than 5 percent of the Fortune 500 CEOs are women, and that statistic drops to 2 percent for the S&P 500 CEOs[1].

Diversity drives business performance. The companies in the top quartile for gender diversity on their executive teams (compared to their fourth-quartile peers) were[2]:

21 percent more likely to experience above average profitability.

33 percent more likely to outperform on profitability (EBIT margin).

27 percent more likely to experience value creation (profit margin).

Yet women only occupy 19 percent of the executive roles in U.S. companies.

What's worse is that telecom, media, and technology companies are disproportionately represented in the fourth-quartile grouping for gender. As if that's not bad enough, they also

---

1   Hunt, Vivian. "Delivering through Diversity." McKinsey&Company, January 2018.
2   Ibid.

saw the greatest *decline* in diversity representation. Tech is headed in the wrong direction!

It gets worse.

In 2018, McKinsey, in partnership with LeanIn.org, performed its fourth Women in the Workplace Study[3]. The findings were...painful.

> "The proportion of women at every level in corporate America has hardly changed [since 2015]. Progress isn't just slow. It's stalled."

> "Women are less likely to be hired into manager-level jobs, and they are far less likely to be promoted into them—for every 100 men promoted to manager, 79 women are. Largely because of these gender gaps, men end up holding 62 percent of manager positions, while women only hold 38 percent."

Over the last four years, many companies have been highly committed to gender diversity, but little progress has been made.

***

I'd invited Dale to lunch. He'd been a long-time mentor and always offered me a great perspective, even if sometimes it hurt. Once I went to complain to him about a nasty email

---

3   Thomas, Rachel. "Women in the Workplace 2018." McKinsey&Co and LeanIn, 2018.

response I had gotten from another department. He had been on copy. I was pissed at the folks who had responded when I walked into his office. I aired my grievances, and he just looked up from his desk and said, "Karen, people who live in glass houses should not throw rocks." I left Dale's office fuming, but a few days later I realized he was totally right. I had thrown the first rock. So that was why I was keen to talk with him: he was always honest and shared his authentic truths. I could trust him to be honest.

Something had been gnawing at me.

While we ate, I told Dale of my growing frustration that women's voices are not heard in business, especially in tech companies. I felt really frustrated, as I have headed up a couple of Diversity & Inclusion efforts, but rarely did we feel we were making an impact.

I shared with him that my fellow women didn't seem able to move the needle and men were not driving change either.

Dale was actually one of my former bosses from General Electric (GE).

I chose him to speak with because I was making a lot of changes and struggling with issues that involved executives, and I knew he had a lot of experience in this arena. Dale had done a lot of work with the GE executive team—not just with our local executives, but also with those at GE's executive training center, fondly known as Crotonville. He wrote the leadership manuals for "Workout!": GE's bureaucracy-busting strategy that was pushed by Jack Welch in his early days at the company. He also spearheaded the CAP (Change Acceleration Program), which was used to change the direction of the massive mothership, GE, back in its glory days. He had worked with Steve Kerr, the infamous leadership expert.

If anyone could help me figure out what was needed to really initiate a change movement, he could. He would know how to get the executives engaged, so we could get this show on the road!

***

"I don't see the problem you are trying to solve."

We've spent nearly an hour talking about the subject and we're still stuck on the opening line!

This statement is from a gentleman I've held in very high regard and who has extensive experience in working with tech executives. He's a very high-EQ individual.

I'm floored.

How can he not see it?

I'm baffled that he can't see it. And he's equally baffled about what exactly is the problem I'm trying to solve.

I thought long and hard after my last lunch with Dale. *Why couldn't he see it? Did I do a crappy job of explaining it? Had he not been exposed to it? What am I missing?*

Then it hit me. *He really, honestly didn't see it. It wasn't that he glanced at it and then looked away choosing to act like he didn't see it.*

It wasn't that he was ignoring it, hoping it would just go away.

He honestly didn't see it.

Then, I had my epiphany:

"Men are really good problem-solvers, but You Can't Fix What You Can't See. Perhaps that's why so little progress is being made!"

***

We have been actively trying to bridge the gender divide since I graduated from college. Yet less than 5 percent of Fortune 500 CEOs are women, and women make up less 19 percent of corporate boards[4]. Even worse, after about twelve years, 50 percent of women with STEM (science, technology, engineering, and math) degrees have left their field and sought employment somewhere else[5].

I have worked in and with engineering for years, and the absolute worst part is losing female coworkers. People have said: "Oh, she wanted to start a family," or "support her kids," or "take care of her parents." I contend that most of those reasons are excuses. Women are too polite to tell you: *I do not feel respected, valued, or listened to. I am watching my male peers*

---

4   Hunt, Vivian. "Delivering through Diversity." McKinsey&Company, January 2018.

5   Ashcraft, Catherine and McLain, Brad and Eger, Elizabeth. "Women in Tech: The Facts; 2016 Update," 2016.

get opportunities and promotions that are not being offered to me. I am not growing and learning as fast as I want to. My suggestions fall on deaf ears. I just don't want to beat my head against this wall anymore. I could be doing something else.

***

Okay, I hear a few of you out there snickering, with a whisper of "maybe those women are not really qualified." Their qualifications are not the problem. I have seen too many perfectly qualified women leave.

So, what *is* the problem?

Ever since I graduated from college, I, as a woman, have been asked to act like a man. My suits had the big shoulder pads; I wore a scarf like a tie. I learned to walked like a man—not intentionally, but their longer legs give them a longer stride, so when walking alongside them, I had to keep up to stay in the conversation. I didn't even know I had adopted this behavior until one of my coworkers pointed it out by saying, "Karen, I always know when you're about to pop into my cube; I can hear you coming from your footsteps. Did you know you have a very distinctive walk?" No, actually, I didn't until someone pointed it out.

I have also been offered all sorts of training to "fix" me to fit into the men's business world. And apparently many women have had the same experience. Assertiveness training, for example, to get women to speak up. Anyone who knows me knows I didn't need this particular class, but many women have been funneled through these courses. Here's a current offering for women's leadership training[6]:

> "Despite years of advances in both legal and corporate policy, many qualified women don't get the jobs they want. Misperceptions, stereotypes, and misplaced emotions on the part of either sex can still sabotage a woman's career hopes—unless she takes a more strategic approach to her career.
>
> "This hands-on leadership course shows women how to strategically use your strengths and abilities—your competitive edge—while mastering your emotions in even the most unwelcoming atmosphere. You'll learn how to build a network of support, take smart risks and view competition in a more positive light. Discover how to conduct yourself in a manner that earns you respect and pursue your goals with positive energy. Return to your job feeling confident, ready to compete fearlessly, and in a better position to be recognized for your true capabilities."

The underlying assumption with these courses is that, to be successful, you must conform to the way men prefer to conduct business. Let me annotate the description above:

---

6 "Leadership Development for Women, Seminar Number: 02010." American Management Association. (Accessed 9/23/2019).

Years of legal and corporate policy changes have not fundamentally changed the way we do business. Women's careers can and will be sabotaged. Such an outcome is clearly not the intention, but it is a byproduct of forcing everyone to conform to a set of unwritten rules that work very well for many men but are stifling and unfair to women.

You can develop your competitive edge. *You know, not everyone thrives on competition, but I guess there's no choice—if we want to be successful, that's what we have to do.*

Master your emotions, even in the most unwelcoming atmosphere. You are obviously too emotional, especially when placed in very difficult environments. *Did it ever occur to people that perhaps it is the environment that needs to change?*

Return to your job feeling confident, ready to compete fearlessly, and in a better position to be recognized for your true capabilities. You must compete fearlessly; that's the only way you can be successful. That's also how Enron happened. We will only recognize those capabilities that have been exhibited by successful men. Other capabilities that don't align with these are unimportant and will not be recognized or respected.

This course description for *Leadership Development for Women* came from the American Management Association Website in August 2019. This is their current training. They are still trying to "fix" women.

This is not a woman problem; it's a business problem for men. Allow me to elaborate. The business world was created by men, for men, and it worked wonderfully for men. Until two things happened: women entered the workforce, and the industrial age was eclipsed by the age of knowledge and all things digital. Now we need to rewrite the rules of business so everyone can fully contribute. And the men need to participate fully in rewriting the rules—it must work for all of us.

***

These facts remain:

Eighty-five percent of women in science, engineering, and technology report "loving their work."[7]

Yet 56 percent leave their organizations between ten and twenty years.[8]

The quit rate for women in science, engineering and technology is much higher than it is for men.

Why do women leave science, engineering, and technology positions? Three major categories were found in a study done by the National Center for Women and Information Technology:[9]

---

7   Ashcraft, Catherine and McLain, Brad and Eger, Elizabeth. "Women in Tech: The Facts; 2016 Update," 2016.
8   Ibid.
9   Ibid.

1. Workplace experiences

2. Lack of access to creative technical roles

3. Dissatisfaction with career prospects

So, how can you "love your work" and then quit? I have spoken with countless women who have done this. The work itself is not the cause—you love that part. It's the 10,000 hurdles put in front of you that aren't actually part of the work but are part of what is needed to get your work done. It's parts of the job like access to the right information or the right people. It's the withholding of information. The caustic remarks. The not being invited to the meeting where decisions are made that impact your work. Honestly, a lot of these feel like intentional sabotage after a while.

> *Just because you're paranoid doesn't*
> *mean they aren't after you.*
>
> —JOSEPH HELLER'S CATCH-22

***

Why did I write this book?

After working in four companies, I have been subjected to a wide variety of insulting, degrading, obnoxious, and humiliating experiences. You will hear about some of these experiences in this book, as well as experiences of other people I know or interviewed as part of my research. These experiences pile up and have been called by others: "death by a thousand paper cuts." They are the loss of opportunities, the not being heard, being shut down (repeatedly), not being given a chance, being interrupted, not being paid fairly, having to prove your competence over and over and over again. It wears you down over time. It makes you disengage.

I find that I can no longer be silent. Many of these deaths by a thousand paper cuts are really the reason I wrote this book. Because I began to understand that many of them seemed invisible to many people. That people were not aware they had even "done" anything, much less aware of the pain they were causing others. The most important reason I wrote this book was when I realized that many of these issues were "fixable." Most often, they are born of ignorance and not malicious intent. When I realized this fact, I decided that the most useful thing I could do with my life was focus on fixing the gender divide.

My three boys are still in school, but perhaps we can fix it, so their life partners and the women of their era don't have to enter a working world like this. If we choose not to act, we are saddling our children with this caustic environment. I want young people to be able to pick the career they want, based on their skill sets, and be successful doing that work. When 50 percent of the women who chose technology careers then leave those careers because of the environment, something is going very wrong. I know that's not the legacy I want to leave for my children. Is that what you want for yours?

Your kids and mine deserve to be respected, valued, and feel like they belong at work. Only then will they be able to deliver their best and be fulfilled, and right now, honestly, that's not happening in the workplace.

So, I set out to write a book that will speed up the process and voice the changes that need to be made, so we can start making some real progress on this issue. Since I believe a big part of the problem is that many people just can't "see" the gender issue, I decided one of my goals must be to give people the power to "see" it clearly and understand how it is negatively impacting our lives, our communities, and most importantly, our businesses.

**

This book explores how our gendered roles have evolved over time. It also looks at how our gendered norms have kept us stuck and frustrated for the last thirty years. But it doesn't stop there: it offers you a framework to really understand some of our key differences in a way that will bring new meaning to your experiences (both past and present). It will give you the power to be able to "see" differently—to interpret actions, behavior, and conversations with a new and more powerful lens.

This book includes the collective wisdom of many well-known experts. It creates a unique intersection from thought leaders and authors as wide-ranging as: Silicon Valley icons like Kim Scott, neuroplasticity expert Dr. Jeffrey Schwartz, gender experts, linguists, innovation experts, business leaders like former *USA Today* Editor-in-Chief Joanne Lipman, *Grit* author Angela Duckworth, leading psychologists like Dr. Daniel Schacter from Harvard University, financial experts like Sallie Krawcheck, and people who have had the opportunity to live on both sides of the gender divide.

***

And Dale, did he finally see it? I solicited his support in editing this book. Through our interactions, he helped me solidify the models presented here to not only help others see the problem but also to apply the models and begin to transform our companies into thriving places where all of our children can honestly be fulfilled.

CHAPTER 1

YOUR SECRET DECODER

―――――

How we interpret a situation decides how we experience it. Create new experiences by thinking differently about what you encounter.

—JERRY CORSTEN

As each of us walks through life, we collect our own unique sets of secret decoders. Rarely do we get a trigger that asks us to go back and ask ourselves if they are currently still working for us. Are they offering us a current truth or are they repeating a message encoded long ago that perhaps needs to be updated? Often, we do not even realize that we carry around a pocket full of these and periodically pull one or many out to interpret the world.

I'd like this chapter to serve as a trigger for you to start looking at your own secret decoders. As you walk through this book, I want you to actually pull your secret decoders out and examine them. For each of them (I know you have many), you should ask yourself the following questions:

- What are the assumptions embedded in this one?
- Do I still believe these assumptions—are they really true, or does evidence indicate that I might want to reconsider and perhaps update or validate whether the assumptions are still valid?
- Is this decoder limiting my choices by saying, "When this happens, do that"? Are there perhaps a plethora of actions I can choose from that are not yet—but should be—encoded in my decoder?

Let's say a particular individual in your office always rubs you the wrong way. You've had many encounters with them and just the sight of them sets you off. You walk into your next meeting and there they are.

You roll your eyes and sigh inwardly, thinking to yourself, *I have to sit here with this jerk for an hour. Nothing positive can possibly come out of this experience, and it's going to be a complete waste of my time.*

This reaction was not prompted by any action from this person other than their presence in the meeting. They have yet to utter a word. Still, your mind has already launched you off, perhaps reacting to a prior encounter, and is busy preparing you for battle.

At this point, it may not matter what this person says; you are prepared to challenge their every comment, and refute any fact that escapes their lips. You have effectively sabotaged any chance of having a productive meeting. None of this response is based on any current evidence, and most of it has happened in your head. Yet, when the meeting progresses and you react as you usually do, the meeting is not productive, and of course you leave blaming that "jerk" for another hour wasted.

In reality, you may have been the one to set the course of the meeting, dooming it from the moment you pulled out your secret decoder about this person. After all, you decided at the beginning that nothing positive could come out of this meeting. That was your assumption going into the meeting. Because of that supposition, you sat in the meeting ready to refute and challenge. Were these the only actions available to you, or could you have pursued other actions? Had you taken a different tack, perhaps he would have shared some evidence that would make you reconsider some of your assumptions. Often the people we sabotage with our decoders are ourselves.

***

You might be wondering why we have secret decoders, where they come from, and what purpose they serve. Our secret decoders are a wonderful creation of our minds that actually allow us to take valuable shortcuts. We are bombarded by all kinds visual, auditory, emotional, and kinesthetic information, and we are incapable of processing it all. So our brains have worked out many shortcuts that allow us to bypass fully processing all this information.

A prime example of such a shortcut is driving. I want you to think back to the days when you first learned to drive. When you first start learning, you are overwhelmed with remembering the mechanisms of driving, while simultaneously trying to recall "the rules of road." At the same time, you are trying to gauge when you should lift your foot from the accelerator and step on the brake as you approach a stop sign. As an experienced driver, you no longer have to think about all these steps. Your brain created many secret decoders for the skill of driving that serve as shortcuts, freeing up your mind to focus on the road while perhaps attempting to remember what you were supposed to pick up on the way home from work.

I inadvertently performed an experiment that allowed me to recall how overwhelming life can be without our secret decoders. I was scheduled to have foot surgery on my right foot. In preparing for this operation, my doctor told me I would not be able to drive for at least six weeks. Then he made an offhand comment: "Although, some people have learned to drive with their left foot."

No way could I survive without driving for six weeks, so I started to practice driving with my left foot several weeks before the surgery. If the doctor hadn't mentioned it, I'm not sure I would have thought about the possibility. I would not have questioned the assumption that I could only drive with my right foot.

I highly encourage you to try this driving experiment (in an empty parking lot without any traffic). You will immediately be taken back to your days as a new driver. I also recommend this test to anyone riding in the car with someone learning to drive. It really helps put the situation in perspective and forces you to understand how overwhelming it can all be.

Our secret decoders are valuable for freeing up our minds so we can focus on other more important information. The only problem is that we are generally not aware we are using our decoders. Even when we create them, we do not sit and think, *What assumptions were present when I created this shortcut?* Nor do we think about whether the assumptions that existed then match the situation to which we currently find ourselves applying these shortcuts. Let's face it: these secret decoders are really so secret, we don't even know when we are using them.

That line makes me recall one of my father's favorite coffee cups, which said:

"My work is so secret that even I don't know what I'm doing."

He worked with military intelligence, but this saying really applies to all of us and our secret decoders.

***

This book includes two major parts: the background and the toolkit.

I included the background information I believe will help most people understand how we got to our current predicament that I call the gender divide. We have been working on this issue for many years, and during this time both blame and shame have been cast about liberally, slathering almost everyone. I don't feel that this approach helps anyone—in fact, it makes people want to duck their heads and crawl back into their caves until the storm blows over.

I do feel that understanding how this issue evolved and what factors contribute to sustaining it are important information to know as we try to unwind the ties that bind us, which is why I include a chapter called "Evolution." This section not only discusses how we evolved over time but also contains some interesting tidbits about gender differences that factored into our evolutionary process. For example, did you know that women have a wider field of vision and men have better depth perception? In this chapter, you'll find out why we evolved this way, along with lots of other interesting evolutionary nuggets.

The other background chapter of the book is about your brain. I have included this information as a primer for the subsequent chapters discussing our differences. In these chapters on differences, I will bring in the work of neuroscientists, behaviorists, psychologists, and other experts to discuss why we do what we do. Some of their explanations may require a basic fundamental understanding of the parts of the brain, what they do, and how they work. So, I included what I thought was the bare minimum of information in the "Your Brain" section so you wouldn't have to look up the basics on your own. You can read this section or use it as a reference source when you feel you need it. Some bits in this chapter can make you look really smart at parties with quips like, "Oh, your mirror neurons made you do that!"

***

The toolkit makes up the remainder of the book. The first section of this portion of the book is dedicated to discussing "Our Differences." This part is broken down into an introduction and three sections about differences. In the introduction, I discuss some key findings that neuroscientists have made regarding how men's and women's brains are wired. These differences form the backbone for the remaining chapters in this portion. Additionally, in this introduction, I introduce the dichotomy scale that will be used throughout the differences section.

Three chapters discuss unique categories of difference. The first involves how we process information or how we each prefer to work. For example, when you first encounter a problem at work, do you prefer to sit and think about it on your own initially or do you prefer to discuss it with a few people first? Each of these styles works, but when people with opposite styles work together you may need to adjust your initial approach to problem-solving to get the best from all people.

The second chapter of this part involves differences in perception. It includes how we perceive information and, perhaps more importantly, how we perceive other people's behavior. There are quite a few shocking statistics in this section. Did you know that when men get angry at work, they actually gain respect—but when women get angry, they suffer a significant loss of respect? In this chapter, many secrets are revealed, including the answer to that age-old question: why is it impossible for some people to ask for directions?

What we value is key to understanding our differences. What we value is important because we use it to establish our own priorities. For example, what's more important to you: accomplishing a task or ensuring that relationships are either built or maintained? How we respond to questions like these allows us to surface some of our core values, which often dictate our behavioral choices. My favorite section in the "Our Differences: Values" chapter is around risk. Did you know that men and women have different reactions to risk? Stressed men become more risk-seeking, while women become more risk-aware. Wouldn't this type of information be particularly handy to know when the pressure is on, the stakes are high, and you are asking your team, "Should we proceed with this action or not?"

***

Women are in a unique position to bring many assets to an organization. The "What Women Offer" chapter highlights these benefits. Did you know that women make 85 percent of consumer purchasing decisions? If your company offers consumer products, do your product development, engineering, marketing, and sales teams include enough women to guide your products in the right direction to meet the needs of this demographic? And then, of course, the question always lingers of whether the women in your organization are actually being heard.

For example, companies with both diversity *and* the ability to leverage that diversity are 45 percent more likely to grow market share and 70 percent more likely to capture new markets. I don't know about you, but I certainly would prefer to work for a company with this capability.

***

At this point in the book, you may be wondering: "Why can't some people see this?" That's the whole impetus for writing this book, so I would be a bit negligent if I didn't address this question. The good news is: we all can develop the ability to see and leverage these differences. It helps if you can identify people who are having trouble seeing and help them see more clearly, because You Can't Fix What You Can't See.

Finally, I wrap it up with a chapter about what you can do. This chapter contains several sections, including what individuals can do, actions for company leadership to consider, and what actions organizations can focus on. Here I also introduce a new framework to leverage gender differences in the workplace. It includes seven steps we can take to transform our two-dimensional secret decoder into a three-dimensional one that allows us to see others perspectives. Also, in this section are the key ingredients for satisfying work and traits that companies with a strong culture should exhibit.

***

This book provides a lot of information about people and their behavior, as well as my own beliefs drawn from a vast amount of research.

- When you successfully combine the talents of men and women, you will capture innovation to drive your business to new heights.
- Women's ambition is different than men's; they seek different things, and you should know what to look for, because it can propel you places you never even dreamed of going!

- Women leave when they are not valued, heard, or respected. We can change this reality, but first we must understand where we are not connecting.

This book offers you an eye-opening experience along with a novel framework to perceive your interactions with others with a different lens. It will allow you to examine and update your secret decoders to be more inclusive.

Reading this book will help you understand at a deeper level what people value and give you tools to facilitate conversations that allow people to belong and be respected for the unique perspectives they bring. You will also find additional information, tools, and links to the podcast on the website: www.YouCantFixWhatYouCantSee.com

As you progress through this book, I'd like to suggest that you identify and write down items that make you curious enough to want to learn more. You should plan to end up with a list of many items. Some of these may be very general, like *why do women apologize so often?* Others may be very specific to you, like why your peer down the hall always manages to piss you off. Keep this list on your phone or in a notebook so you can handily record while you read, but also as you go about your day. We will come back to your list in the last chapter.

Diversity is one of the most powerful forces available to accelerate your business. To leverage diversity, two components are required. First, you must have the diversity represented in all areas of your company. Second, you must be able to leverage that diversity. Leveraging that diversity (often called inclusion) is what this book is all about. It requires a shift in your culture and a different perspective. And once you start "seeing" this problem and discussing it as part of your culture, you will open the floodgates of innovation, market growth, and engagement.

CHAPTER 2

EVOLUTION

It always seems impossible until it's done.

—NELSON MANDELA

LONG, LONG AGO

The way we behave today is rooted in millions of years of history.

Neanderthals were believed to be nomadic, and men and women supposedly performed a lot of the same tasks in that era. A large divide in the tasks done by each gender may not have existed.

Homo sapiens then emerged and initially survived much as the Neanderthals had. Life was hard. The focus was on two main areas: protect yourself from predators and find enough food to survive.

The men became strong and began to take over the hunting. Much of this behavior was individual. You can't take twenty people hunting as a group; you'll spook the game. The men did hunt in groups but were not necessarily together.

You can imagine the men finding the game they want to hunt, then making their plan:

"You start here and run that way; I'll run this way, and we'll chase these animals over the cliff. He'll wait at the bottom of the cliff with a big club. We'll all work together to drag the meat back to our cave."

It was an isolated togetherness. Men's brain architecture evolved to screen out peripheral thoughts, focus their attention, and make step-by-step decisions. Power for men became defined by physical strength and the ability to secure the game, which required a lot of focus. To hunt game, you need to perceive, then act quickly. These skills became more highly refined in men as did the pattern: perceive, then act.

The women were constantly pregnant or raising children. They stayed closer to home to care for the little ones and gathered in groups because there was protection in numbers. They took on the task of foraging and gathering food. Since they were together, women created and protected the community. As a result, female brain development began to shift to accommodate the tasks women needed to accomplish.

Helen Fisher gave a great description of the female agenda in that era in her book *The First Sex:*[10]

"In order to rear helpless infants, ancestral mothers needed to do a lot of things at the same time. Watch for snakes. Listen for thunder, taste for poison, rock the sleepy. Distract the cranky. Instruct the curious. Soothe the fearful, inspire the tardy. Feed the hungry. Mothers had to do countless daily chores while they stoked the fire, cooked the food, and talked to friends."

Women's brains evolved to multitask, build social connections, and read social cues based on the environment they had to survive in. Other skills that women honed drove their brains to evolve differently. Women developed a keener sense of intuition. Why? Have you ever tried to calm down an inconsolable child? Or figure out what a crying baby needs? Intuition helps people figure out the answers to such problems. Intuitive people are outstanding at observing their surroundings and sensing both their own and other people's feelings. They are also quite good at picking up inconsistencies people are exhibiting, e.g., what people are saying versus what their body language is communicating.

---

10   Fisher, Helen. *The First Sex; the Natural Talents of Women and How They are Changing the World*, Ballantine Books, 2000.

The women in a community were together most of the time during this era. They worked together. A different sense of hierarchy and values developed as a result. A different organizational or power structure became important to the women. They needed to have both harmony and trust. They needed to understand where the other women were coming from. Maintaining the social structure became more important for women. Developing harmonious connections was critical to their survival and the survival of their families. This became the power structure for women.

"Women are built for mind reading," Fisher explained. "Touch, hearing, smell, taste, vision: all of women's senses are in some respects, more finely tuned than those of men. Women also have a knack for decoding your emotions by looking at your face. They swiftly decipher your mood from your body posture and gestures."

After all, if you are going to leave your baby with the others while you gather the special berries needed for a ceremony, you have to sure they'll protect your child.

This division of labor driven by two different sets of survival needs began the gender divide millions of years ago.

If you're wondering how this evolutionary history might manifest itself in today's world, Daniel Schacter, chair of Harvard University's department of psychology, wrote this in his book *The Seven Sins of Memory*:[11]

---

11 Schacter, Daniel L. *The Seven Sins of Memory; How the Mind Forgets and Remembers. Mariner Books*, 2002.

"Consider one evolutionary hypothesis about memory noted in the article by Buss and coworkers: women have more accurate memories for the spatial locations of objects than men do. The Canadian psychologists Marion Eals and Irwin Silverman suggest that men engaged primarily in hunting whereas women primarily foraged. They hypothesized that these different activities placed different demands on spatial cognition and memory. Successful foragers must locate food sources that are embedded within complex arrays of vegetation and remember those locations for later visits. Natural selection therefore should have favored the development of superior memory for the spatial location of objects in women compared to men.

"They tested this hypothesis and women remembered the locations of objects more accurately than men did. But men outperformed women on other spatial tasks that according to Eals and Silverman, men tap spatial abilities that would have been required for successful hunting. Some studies have replicated these results, whereas others have placed various qualifications and limitations on the findings. The question of whether spatial memory abilities in women are adaptations produced by selection for foraging skills is accordingly, not yet settled."

As we evolved, communities became larger, allowing people to specialize their skills. We figured out how to plant crops instead of just gathering what was available. Others built shelters, prepared food, fashioned clothing for warmth and ceremonies. Some specialized in healing the sick. Societies became more efficient and could thus support larger communities and even more specialization.

Men and women lived together but did not "work" side by side in this era. They primarily worked in their own groups. Each group had its own power structures and values.

Differences continued to emerge. Women developed some keener senses. These include hearing, tasting, and even peripheral vision. Women prepared the food. They protected the group from spoiled food and natural toxins. Women can taste sweet, sour, salty, and bitter flavors in lower concentrations.

"Women also have keener peripheral vision," Fisher wrote. "Because of the way the eyeball is constructed, men are slightly better at depth perception while women have a somewhat wider field of vision."[12]

These differences make a lot of sense when you consider that women were out foraging for food. They needed not only to see the plants they were looking for, but also to keep an

---

12   Fisher, Helen. *The First Sex; the Natural Talents of Women and How They are Changing the World*, Ballantine Books, 2000.

eye out for predators. Men needed depth perception to help them throw the spear accurately to hit the game in the bush.

According to Fisher, the invention of the plow was the trigger that began to change the power balance between men and women.[13]

"The plow. This implement would be as important to the growth of civilization as the harnessing of fire, the development of the printing press, the invention of the steam engine and the creation of the computer chip," Fisher's book reads. "But it would destroy the balance of power between women and men. With the emergence of the plow and the domestication of animals for work and transport, men began to turn away from hunting to fell the trees, plow the fields, irrigate the plants, tend and harvest crops and cart the extra produce off to local markets. Men also became obliged to defend their precious land."

Men became the primary producers. Soon they owned their own land, livestock, and crops, which they converted to wealth and influence. The role of women, of course, had to shift too. They developed new skills such as spinning and weaving, tending to the family livestock, and other domestic work like making soap, bread, and candles. They also

---

13   Ibid.

began rearing more children to help work the land and do the chores.

No longer did the women roam, collecting needed goods and trading their wares with their neighbors and those in further flung communities. Their pursuit of trading luxury items and sharing information far and wide was set aside. Their bargaining chips of power and prestige that had come from supporting the household and bringing home much of the food were gone.

"As women lost the essential leverage to bargain, their status plummeted"[14]

Women were suddenly deemed inferior to men.

You must realize that, at this point in time, perhaps around 10,000 years ago, no formal education really existed. Everything was passed down from the community to the children vicariously. Women, collectively, spent many centuries in this inferior position to men.

Eventually, around the 1600s, more formal types of education started to emerge. By this time, the inferiority of women placed them lowest on the totem pole as recipients of this education, which served to keep them in the inferior position for another couple of centuries.

---

14   Ibid.

But women faced another obstacle as well: pregnancy.

THE EVOLUTION OF BIRTH CONTROL

We owe a great deal to Margaret Sanger[15], but many do not understand the freedom she has offered to women, families, and the workplace.

Margaret Sanger was born in 1879, when times were quite a bit different from today. Sometimes it helps to look back at where we've been to understand where we are now. The path forward can be shaped by this context, and you can frequently avoid future obstacles using this hindsight knowledge.

Margaret's father, Michael Higgins, immigrated to the United States from Ireland when he was fourteen and joined the Army as a drummer during the Civil War. He studied medicine and phrenology but became a stonecutter. He was a free thinker who eventually became an atheist and an activist for women's suffrage and free public education.

Margaret's mother, Anne Higgins, was also from Ireland and married Michael in 1869. She had eighteen pregnancies, resulting in eleven live births over the span of twenty-two years. Her mother died at the young age of forty. In this era, no birth control was available. Women just had a succession of children, many who died early, only to be succeeded as

---

15   Nunez-Eddy, Claudia and Lakshmeeramya, Malladi "Margaret Higgins Sanger (1879-1966)," The Embryo Project Encylopedia. (Accessed Feb 18, 2018).

a result of the next pregnancy. When Margaret was eight, she helped deliver one of her siblings. Margaret was the sixth of eleven surviving children and spent a good deal of her early years helping her mom raise her siblings.

When Margaret was growing up, she saw the horrid living conditions of poor Irish factory workers living along the river in Corning, New York. She attributed happiness to small families and unhappiness to large families. Her early years had a profound impact on her, and she went on to study nursing. While training to be a nurse, Margaret was often called to homes to assist physicians with births. The "soon-to-be" mothers begged for information to prevent future pregnancies. Abstinence was the only cure that Margaret was aware of in the early 1900s.

Margaret worked with immigrant families in which women had many children and miscarriages. These women had no access to information about how to avoid pregnancy, so they also had self-induced abortions. You could only feed so many—it was the grim reality of those times.

When Margaret was twenty-five, her mother's sister gave birth to an unwanted baby. They tossed the newborn into a snowbank; they could not feed another child. Margaret Sanger pulled her niece from the snowbank and took her inside. That moment was the start of a long relationship and the beginning of the Wonder Woman story.

Margaret joined the Socialist Party, and her activist career began when she filled in for a missing speaker addressing a small group of ten women from the party. She spoke about women's health. The next time she was scheduled to speak, seventy-five people showed up—clearly, women wanted to know more. So Margaret started writing a series of articles titled "What Every Mother Should Know," which mothers could use to educate their children about reproduction. Her second series, "What Every Girl Should Know," taught about female reproduction from puberty to menopause. One article from the later series that discussed gonorrhea and syphilis, both sexually transmitted diseases, was charged with violating the 1873 Comstock Act. This act gave the U.S. Post Office the power to censor material in the mail for obscene or sexually explicit language.

In 1912, Margaret gave up her career as a nurse to help women control when they became pregnant. She spent a year studying contraception. In France, she discovered that citizens used family planning and contraception and that the French government did not ban this information. Margaret helped educate people both through her speeches and her writing. She communicated her "why" well, with this story:

"Sadie Sachs had become extremely ill from a self-induced abortion; Margaret and her Doctor nursed her back to health. After Sadie was better, she pleaded with the Doctor to tell her how she could prevent this from happening in the future. Abstinence was the Doctors only answer. A few months later Margaret was called back to Sadie's home. Another abortion gone bad, only this time it took Sadie's life. Imagine how Margaret felt that day while she watched Sadie die, helpless to change the outcome."

Margaret was driven by her life experience and the tales of woe brought to her through her nursing career. She wanted women to have a more equal footing and healthier lives. She believed that if women could choose when and when not to have children, their lives would be significantly improved. This development would also eliminate the need for self-induced abortions, saving many women's lives.

On one of her return trips from Europe, Margaret decided to start a magazine called *The Women Rebel*, which focused on helping working women and emphasized their rights. In this publication, she first used and coined the phrase "birth control." She advertised this magazine in newspapers and got hundreds of subscriptions. The first issue was published in March 1914, but the Post Office told her it was in violation of the Comstock Act. She continued to try and publish it anyway, leaving out information about contraceptives, but the Post Office banned the May and July issues as well.

Later in 1914, she published a pamphlet titled "Family Limitation," which included all the information about contraceptives, such as spermicide, that she had learned in

France. As the Post Office began formal legal proceedings against Margaret, she fled the country to avoid prosecution while she constructed her defense. Margaret returned to the country when one of her three children was dying from pneumonia. Because of the death of her child, the organization dropped the charges against her.

Two years later, Margaret and her sister, Ethel, opened the first birth control clinic in New York. Women circled the street, paying ten cents to consult with a nurse. It only remained open for nine days before the police arrested Margaret for distributing information on contraception. When the judge convicted her, he wrote that women did not have "the right to copulate with a feeling of security that there will be no resulting conception."

Margaret would be arrested eight more times. She traveled to Europe and brought back diaphragms. She continued to speak, write, and push to change the laws that restricted the discussion of contraception and family planning. She founded the modern birth control movement.

Margaret had a lot of support for her vision. She and her first husband divorced in 1914. When he returned to the United States from Europe after the divorce, he was arrested for distributing the "Family Limitation" pamphlet. Her ex-husband chose to serve one month in jail to support her cause to legalize information on contraception. Her second husband smuggled diaphragms into the United States from Canada, driving them over the border in boxes marked "3 in

1 Oil." Later, he would also become the first manufacturer of diaphragms in the United States.

Margaret believed that when women were liberated from the risk of unwanted pregnancy, social change could occur, and the status of women would improve. She launched a campaign to stop the government censorship of contraceptive information. In 1918, her efforts began to pay off, when the New York Court of Appeals issued a ruling allowing doctors to prescribe contraception.

Margaret was relentless: this movement was her life's calling, and she pursued it with vigor, even deploying unconventional tactics. She ordered diaphragms from Japan, using the anticipated government confiscation to launch a legal battle, which resulted in a 1936 court decision to overturn provisions of the Comstock Law that prohibited physicians from obtaining contraceptives. As a result, in 1937, the American Medical Association adopted contraception as a normal medical service and began teaching it in medical school. The organization she founded became the Planned Parenthood we know today, and she served as its leader until she was in her 80s.

Margaret eventually saw her dream come true. She got a philanthropist to fund efforts to develop "the pill." The FDA approved its use in 1960. Then, in 1965, the U.S. Supreme Court made birth control legal, but only for married couples. In 1966, Margaret Sanger passed away, leaving a legacy today that has touched each of our lives in ways we cannot even imagine.

THE THREE SECRETS OF WONDER WOMAN

Margaret Sanger is Wonder Woman for today's women, their families, and the organizations where they work. She fundamentally changed the world for us. Her Wonder Woman characteristics can be summarized in three strengths that each of us can emulate.

The first step in becoming Wonder Woman is to have a vision of a better world.

Margaret's life experiences drove her vision. She served as a nurse for immigrant families and had to watch helplessly as women died from self-induced abortions. She watched families suffer as more children were born than could be fed. Her vision evolved into birth control, which has freed women and families to decide when having children is right for their lives. This development allowed women to entertain a "career" while significantly reducing the need for abortions.

The second step to becoming Wonder Woman is perseverance. Keep chipping away at the bad guys, regardless of what they throw at you. She was arrested nine times and thrown in jail, yet she started several movements and just did not give up. She even used the antiquated laws to start legal battles, so the legality and morality of the laws could be contested in court.

She made amazing accomplishments in just one lifetime and significantly improved the trajectory of women for human history. But there's more to this story.

The baby she pulled from the snowbank was Olive Byrne, her niece. Olive grew up near Margaret and was influenced not just by her causes, but also by her strength of character and willpower. Olive would grow up with Margaret and her mother Ethel as her role models. Olive ended up attending Tufts University where William Marston was teaching and became his research assistant. William was married to his wife Elizabeth; they were both psychologists and very non-traditional in many ways. William brought Olive home one day and told his wife she would be living with them. It was a ménage à trois arrangement that worked so well the two women cohabitated for another 50 years—after his death.

Many do not know that William Marston was the creator of Wonder Woman. His lasting creation of the first female superhero was no accident. He firmly believed he was living with two Wonder Women and shaped the cartoon image from the physical characteristics of both Olive and Elizabeth. Olive loved to wear very wide bracelets on both arms, which became the signature of Wonder Woman's costume.

Margaret remained close to her niece, Olive, and her influence showed up in the feminist ideals of the comic. You see, the creator of Wonder Woman had a profound belief that women possessed incredible power, power that could change the world. And that is the third step to becoming a Wonder Woman. Change the world for the better, which Margaret and Wonder Woman certainly did.

THE INDUSTRIAL AGE

The era of education coincided with the beginning of the Industrial Age. Our communities were larger, allowing people to specialize further and focus on very specific areas to bring efficiencies into play. Many inventions began to change the way in which work was done.

The gender divide was ever-present. Typically, men left their homes to tend to their work and women stayed at home to care for children, who occupied the home for much longer than we see now, due to the lack any reliable method of birth control.

Women continued to build the communities. They formed their own way of getting things done. Preserving relationships and community was more important than accomplishing individual tasks. But times were changing. Women began getting educated; they even began securing college degrees.

World War II broke out in 1939, and circumstances had to change. Men were needed to fight the war; women had to enter the workforce. Someone had to run the local businesses and supply the many items needed to support the war effort. Women found that they excelled working outside the home. They used their connections and communities to handle their newly emerged dual roles as workers and mothers. Someone still had to take care of the younger children, and these relationships proved invaluable toward that goal.

Nearly nineteen million women were working during World War II. The government ran many campaigns encouraging housewives to enter the workforce, and also found it needed to run campaigns to convince the women's husbands to allow them to take on these jobs.

Many men and even some women were trained in the military way of thinking: command and control. This management model worked well. The leaders accumulated knowledge and rose to the top of the organization. This model was created by men and fine-tuned to how their brains had evolved to work: compartmentalize, focus on a task or goal, and execute.

Finally, the war was over. Everything could return to normal—or so people thought.

The women were let go as the men returned home. The men took their jobs back and fathered the Baby Boom generation. A quiet but significant change had occurred. Provisions had been made for others to take care of the children while women worked in the factories, powering the war machine and provisioning their local communities. Women had found new skills, and many reveled in the personal challenge of accomplishments outside the home. Women had tasted this new sense of fulfillment. The Rosie the Riveter saying "We can do it" became internalized for many as "I did it, and it felt great"; new horizons began to open for women.

Shortly after the war ended, another major pivot occurred. Birth control became widely available. Women and families now had a choice about having children and could control the timing of when this miracle of life occurred.

For a time, people thought everything had returned to normal, mainly because of the birth of the baby boomers. But that status quo was not to last. Just like a tent neatly rolled in its original packaging, you will find that, once unrolled, you can never quite stuff it back into the original box. It had expanded. So too had women, freed from a life of continuous childbirth and child-rearing, awakened to the world of having a career; their horizons blossomed.

Prosperity in the United States was at an all-time high, and it continued to accelerate. The Industrial Age modernized the home life: washing machines, dishwashers, and vacuums proliferated, and even televisions were invented, seemingly to fill the free time created by our new, more efficient households. The *Happy Days* era was a glorious time. The expectation that you would be better off than your parents' generation had become a reality for many.

***

The science of management was born during the Industrial Age. It was built around the command-and-control model that had successfully powered us through the war years. This war model works well when someone is shooting at you and you need to deploy thousands of people and equipment to a specific area in a short time. Having detailed plans, rule books, and people who followed orders was required.

Public companies took this model to heart, deciding it must be the way to run an efficient company. Keep in mind that this was also the era when the boss had worked his way up through the ranks. Managers knew the details of most jobs because they had worked in many of these jobs. They had "done their time." The most knowledgeable people in the company rose to the top. These leaders formulated the strategies and plans that were passed down through the ranks to be executed by the troops.

Women began to take education seriously, and more and more of them were earning college degrees and entering the workforce. No longer did marriage mean babies. They could put off starting a family until they were ready. In 1978, the number of women earning associate (two-year) degrees exceeded that of the men. In 1982, women earned more bachelor's degrees than their male counterparts. It took another five years for women to surpass men in securing master's degrees. The tipping point of women securing more doctorate degrees took two more decades but was reached in 2006, according to the U.S. Department of Education.[16]

---

16   Kirst, Michael W. "Women Earn More Degrees than Men: Gap Keeps Increasing," The College Puzzle – Stanford, May 28, 2013. (Accessed June 2019).

***

I graduated in 1981 with a bachelor's degree in mechanical engineering, just a year before the number of bachelor's degrees earned by women exceeded that earned by men. Engineering was not the typical degree choice for a woman, but I had always been different. In seventh grade, I invented a perpetual motion machine. My science teacher told me it was impossible, but I didn't care. You see, my mother had taught me that I could do anything I was willing to put the effort into. I could be anyone I really wanted to be. I believed her.

I had another advantage as well. I came from a family that revered education. Three of my grandparents had college degrees, and the one who didn't was a businessman and an entrepreneur. I had no idea that this situation was highly unusual for that era. It was my normal.

Although I was raised in California, I went to high school in Alabama. I remember my classmates asking me what I planned to do after high school. I told them I was going to college to get an engineering degree. Many just looked at me with a very confused and questioning look on their face. They seemed to be screaming, *Why?* I didn't understand the depth of that question until much, much later.

As it turned out, many girls in my high school had only one aspiration in life: to get married, settle down, and start a family. Their big goal was to score that engagement ring during high school. Then they would be set for life. The next big question would be whether they would move into a trailer behind his parents' house, or hers.

I was having none of that. I had watched my mother struggle after my parents divorced, trying to make ends meet, trying to get society to accept her as an individual and not a 'divorcee'. Back then divorce was an awful stigma, you were marked as 'not normal', and treated as if you wore the Scarlet Letter. My mom had her own career as a Physical Therapist and had had her own practice while she was married. I was going to have my own career to ensure that I could always take care of myself.

I was fascinated by engineering. It was fun. You got to solve all kinds of problems; that's what I wanted to do. When I went to college, I stayed on the top floor of the dorm during my first year. This floor was dedicated to female engineering students. We had several advisers on the floor, older engineering students who could help you out with homework when you got stuck. I was very lucky to have landed in such a supportive environment, because college was not easy. I spent most of my time studying. I didn't really have time to party, like many other students. Plus, I had to work to cover some of my expenses. Having that dedicated engineering floor of the dorm helped set me on the right track. We studied together, which made it easier and set me up with habits that would help me succeed even after I left the dorm.

I entered the workforce, joining General Electric Company (GE), and returning to California. At this point, the song "Do You Know the Way to San Jose" came to have real meaning—because no one did. It was before the valley was really known for silicon; it was better known for its orchards and fruit production at that time.

This was the GE just before Jack Welch. At the time, GE was legendary for creating systems and processes to run companies like clockwork. It had created the GE "blue books" in the 1950s. These were operating procedures that spelled out everything management needed to do (and I mean *everything*). These blue books represented the latest in scientific thinking applied to management. These procedures were created at GE's legendary training facility, Crotonville, by then-CEO Ralph Cordiner, with the help of the infamous Peter Drucker.

Other companies were in awe of GE's management ability and frequently tried to copy its techniques. In the '60s, GE created the science around strategic planning. Then, in the '80s, Jack Welch launched Work-Out, GE's bureaucracy-busting program, designed to force the leadership team to become more candid, flexible, and nimble.

"Despite their differences, Mr. Cordiner and Mr. Welch held the same core idea about organizational change: the only way to shift a company's culture is to change the habitual thinking and behavior of its fast-track executives," strategy expert Art Kleiner explained.[17]

I joined the nuclear power division of GE just two years after the Three Mile Island accident. The company was still frantically starting up plants that had been ordered and were already under construction at the time of the accident. Our leadership team spoke of a "lull" in new plant orders. Truth is, no one would order a new plant for at least twenty more years, and it would not be for a plant in the United States.

I joined the GE engineering training program, somewhat of an exclusive group of people recruited out of college who would be brought in and trained in the ways of GE management. We were expected to be groomed as the future leaders of the company. We took four six-month rotational assignments in a variety of functions while we studied some very nuclear-industry-specific engineering concepts. Little did we realize that some of the problems we were asked to solve were given to us because the answers did not yet exist. The thinking was:

"These young engineers are the best and brightest. Let's see if they can solve these problems."

At the end of two years, we could attend University of California at Berkeley to complete our master's degrees in engineering. This era was when GE grew its own talent.

---

17   Colvin, Geoffrey; "What Makes GE Great?" CNN Money, Feb 24, 2006.

BIRTH OF THE SERVICE BUSINESS

Without realizing it, I landed in the birthplace of the GE engineering services business. It was a small group formed to help customers with problems they were having with the operation of their plants. We would do engineering analysis to figure out what was happening and then recommend solutions. Frequently, the solutions required an amendment to their operating license, and we would need to justify the changes with the Nuclear Regulatory Commission. Sometimes the problems were unique to one plant, but often several plants experienced similar problems. Once we recognized this fact, we could help other plants improve their operations too.

Most of what we did had not been done before. It required combining the knowledge and talents of specialists from all over the division, which was not the way GE was designed to operate. The command-and-control management model was designed to compartmentalize knowledge for efficiency. We always worked across these compartments—we had to; a nuclear power plant was a complicated integrated system. You couldn't fiddle in one area without impacting the whole system. So, I learned to navigate in spite of the organizational structure.

GE was changing too. Jack Welch had taken over just a few months after I started work there. It took quite a while for some of his philosophies to show up in San Jose. We were a somewhat isolated and often overlooked part of the company. We did not fit the standard manufacturing model of the rest of GE. Quite frankly, the company did not know what to do with our division, so we were mostly left to our own devices, a fact I learned to be grateful for.

***

Jack believed the company had become too bureaucratic, and he was right. Our division, however, got an early start in retooling our business. After all, necessity is the mother of invention, and a huge chunk of our revenue stream from new plants had simply disappeared after the Three Mile Island accident. We were lucky in that there was a huge backlog we had yet to deliver, but we also had to fill in the revenue hole, and we did it by creating a services business. The business was built based on our customers' needs. We designed services to solve their problems and make the plants run more efficiently, saving our customers millions of dollars and eliminating many headaches for them.

To make a nuclear plant more efficient, you had to look at the entire plant. Initially, we focused on the nuclear side, but we also had to branch out into the turbine and generator part of the plant. I was put in charge of trying to get our GE counterparts back in Schenectady, New York, to understand what we were trying to do.

It was then, when I ran face-first into the impenetrable wall of bureaucracy, that I realized and became grateful for our isolation from the rest of the company.

We lived by serving our customers and understanding what they were trying to accomplish. The turbine group lived to serve their management team, as near as I could tell. It was incredibly frustrating. While we worked for the same company, we were light-years apart.

When programs like Work-Out[18] landed on our doorstep, we embraced them. We had grown tired of fighting the bureaucracy and the silos. Work-Out was a program Jack rolled out early in his CEO tenure. It used the power of the individual to undo bureaucracy. Groups of employees were gathered together for a day and brainstormed to identify bureaucracy to eliminate. At the end of the session, the leadership team gathered to hear the ideas. They had to decide then and there what to eliminate. It was a very empowering program. In fact, one of my mentors, Dale, wrote the facilitators manual. He told me the hardest part was coaching the management team. Many managers were horrified that they would be asked to decide to eliminate "sacred cows." Even worse, they would be asked to do this "on the spot," in a public meeting.

***

18   Kleiner, Art; "GE's Next Workout," PwC Strategy & Business, Issue 33, Winter 2003.

Many people go to great lengths to tell you that you need to plan your career out and follow the plan. While to some extent I agree, there a lot of things you simply can't plan or you wouldn't prioritize that turn out much later to have great significance in your life.

I was offered a "stretch" assignment. At GE, these assignments were how you grew your leadership pipeline. Once you had proven yourself technically competent, you were then given opportunities to take on additional responsibilities. These frequently took the form of additional projects piled on top of your "day job." I was asked to co-lead the first GE Diversity Council. At the time, I thought, *What is diversity?* and *Why would I waste my precious engineering time to figure it out?* This was the later part of the '80s, when, honestly, we didn't know how to spell diversity or understand why it mattered. Don't get me wrong: we had a fairly culturally diverse workforce and many female engineers. We also had a lot of international clients as our plants were operating around the world. We talked to a lot of people and put on cultural fairs to help understand cultural differences.

I co-led the council for a few years. Then I realized that everything to do with diversity was landing in the collective lap of the council. We were dealing with a lot, gaining a lot of knowledge, and becoming a great resource. But our leadership team was not learning a thing. They kicked everything our way, abdicating their responsibility. Those in leadership were not becoming more knowledgeable, gaining awareness, or even understanding the issues.

At this time, if you picked up the GE annual report, you would see picture after picture of men who all looked very similar. The leadership team had little to no diversity, although our division contained quite a lot of diversity in the rank-and-file teams. In our second year, the Diversity Council went to the president of our division and we collectively quit. The team had a few tense meetings before agreeing on this decision. We carefully explained that our existence was preventing leadership from doing the work that they needed to personally do. Such a move was bold. At the time, I was quite convinced that this act would do some serious damage to our careers, but sometimes you just have to do what you feel is right.

* * *

As I moved up the management chain and took on more responsibility, I found myself engaging more with customers, partners, and our leadership team. I had several encounters with both our management and customers that had left me stunned.

What exactly are you supposed to do when a high-level customer asks you to go to bed with them while you are in the middle of negotiating contracts worth millions of dollars?

Neither my engineering background nor my leadership training had prepared me to respond to these advances. To say it was overwhelming, confusing, and made me feel inadequate would be a major understatement. The experience was embarrassing and humiliating. I never told a soul; I certainly did not want to relive any part of it. It happened numerous times. The incidents passed. And, each time, I kept my silence.

THE INFORMATION AGE

Knowledge became more widely disseminated. Information exploded—understanding all aspects of a technology, much less a company, was no longer possible. The Information Age had begun. Women in the workforce became commonplace.

Women brought unique skills and perspectives into the workforce. They excelled at relationships and building communities where all could contribute their best. They could see more possibilities and were able to connect concepts inside broad swaths of evolving industries and even across industries. But they found it hard to get ahead in corporate America. The folks in management did not really see their talent. Clearly, when judged by the existing standards, women did not fit the mold of "corporate success." They were different. They did not act like the men.

This era was fraught with the paradigm that if women could be trained to act like men, they would fit in and could take their place in the workforce. I wore suits to work, typically with a scarf around my neck that looked suspiciously like a tie. Our jackets and even blouses had shoulder pads to make us appear to have broad shoulders, just like the men. Assertiveness training classes for women flourished. Lucky for me, I was born with that inclination anyway, and entering the workforce in nuclear power and being surrounded by ex-Navy nukes solidified it.

I watched women bring up new ideas that first hit deaf ears, then crashed to the floor. I also watched competitors move forward with something very similar and proceed to eat our lunch. We now enter an age of dawning realization. Neuroscience has done a lot to explain that we really are different—while also opening our eyes to understand brain plasticity, busting the old adage that you can't teach an old dog new tricks. But we continue to manage the workplace with a command-and-control mentality.

To me, this approach is like trying to wear a pair of pants that is simply too small. They crush your midsection, making it hard to breathe, the legs hit you midcalf, leaving you exposed to hungry mosquitoes, and you can't bend over for fear of splitting your back seam open. Something that tight doesn't even make you look good. Ten pounds of potatoes in a five-pound bag just doesn't cut it. You simply can't work dressed this way. It's not even functional. That's what the command-and-control workplace felt like. It's also the impact it frequently has on the organization: It's confining.

It squelches any thoughts of creativity. It minimizes any cross-functional communication.

We need to rewrite the rules for work in a way that leverages differences in people rather than judging them. The new rules must also accommodate the Information Age in which we now live. Understanding everything is no longer possible; the world has gotten too complicated. You must rely on experts from many disciples and they, in turn, must be able to interact to generate cross-functional solutions we need. We must be able to rely on our teams.

To do this, we need to understand the differences and create new norms that allow everyone to flourish, thus we also have to be able to converse about our differences. Here, I am talking about differences in how we process information, perceive the world, and what we personally value. How often do these conversations take place in your workplace?

The nature of our work has changed dramatically, as has the makeup of our workforce, but the method of management is mired in the past. The time has come to open up our minds and consider new models. When we can leverage the qualities of all parts of our workforce, we will truly be able to unleash innovation and market growth, and that will drive engagement to new highs. It becomes a self-sustaining upward spiral.

CHAPTER 3

YOUR BRAIN

———

How can a three-pound mass of jelly that you can hold in your palm imagine angels, contemplate the meaning of infinity, and even question its own place in the cosmos?[19]

—V.S. RAMACHANDRAN

We are driven by many forces we often just don't understand. A lot of what happens in our minds falls below our ability to detect, and frequently we feel many of these things are outside of our control. In the last twenty years or so, we have just started to really understand our brains and how they function. However, if you were to look back on today twenty years from now, we will probably be saying, "Oh, we

———

19 Ramachandran, VS. The Tell-Tale Brain: A Neuroscientist's Quest for What Makes Us Human. W.W. Norton & Company, 2012.

were Neanderthal in our thinking twenty years ago." Evolution has also given us multiple layers of brain functionality, which we are only just beginning to understand.

In addition, some things many of us believe to be true in fact are not. Neuroplasticity is a prime example of something we thought for years was not possible but has been there all along, staring us right in the face.

Your brain also contains your many secret decoders, those shortcuts your brain uses to prevent information overload. Keep in mind, we don't consciously create these, and most of the time we don't even know they are there or that we're using them. We use them as a time-saver. No need to figure this problem out; just pull out the "how to deal with a person begging on the street" card and follow the steps. It offers an easy shortcut.

We have a lot of homeless people in our area who ask for money at intersections. One day, a young woman stood at the freeway off-ramp. I pulled my secret decoder out: make no eye contact, stare straight ahead. The sign she was holding said she had three kids. My son rolled down the window and asked her how old her kids were. She told him they were just a little younger than my three boys. She asked if maybe we had some old clothes they had outgrown that her kids could wear. The light turned green, but my son called out that we'd be back.

We went home and collected some of their outgrown things, found an old suitcase, and my boys packed it with the clothes, adding some toys and books as well. We must have driven by that location for a week, before we finally saw her again. We gave her the suitcase, and she was thrilled. She said her three boys would love the toys and books. Everyone felt great after our exchange. My son bypassed my "how to deal with a person begging on the street" card and taught me a valuable lesson: sometimes you need to look at your secret decoder and see when and if you really want to use it. Maybe you do need to do a little analysis to figure out what you should do. Perhaps your secret decoder has a few assumptions that need validating. As you go through your day, think about your secret decoders as you use them.

Some brain actions are almost involuntary. Our response to some stimuli, such as a saber-toothed tiger appearing in front of us, will trigger our fight, flight, or freeze response. We have this response to protect us; it is part of our reptilian brain. The problem is that, in most offices, saber-toothed tigers roam no longer, but that response is still there. When we feel like we are under attack (the trigger), our brains respond to protect us. Many times, our innate reaction, our first response, is not actually helping us.

Imagine me as a young engineer. I was asked to give a presentation to one of our general managers. Let's call him Fred. It was a very important presentation, with which I was to secure his approval for a simplified business process for performing small consulting jobs for our customers. At the time, we were required to use a very complicated process designed to sell multimillion-dollar packages. Needless to say, it was overly cumbersome for a $50,000-contract and seriously hurting our business. These small contracts usually helped us diagnose problems and thus provided us the needed information to propose work that would then remedy the problem. If we couldn't get the first contract in place while customers were hot for a fix, we'd never get to the second contract.

Fred had quite a reputation, in many areas. I was lucky I had several weeks to prepare for my presentation. Numerous people coaching me and reviewing my drafts shared the stories they had either experienced or witnessed. Turns out, Fred had trouble controlling his temper and was also known as a womanizer. One of the most frightening stories that I was told, by more than one person, concerned the fate of an engineer who had presented something Fred did not agree with. At the tensest part of the meeting, Fred stood up and threw a hot cup of coffee, cup and all, at the poor guy. I spent a lot of time pondering what my fate would be, as a woman, trying to get a controversial change approved by him.

Honestly, knowing all this information did not help me prepare for this presentation. Fred's reptilian—innate—response served as a major distraction during my preparation, as fearing for your life (or at least the life of your suit) does not put your brain on the innovative and creative path needed to define and get new processes approved. I wondered, How many people just chose to stay silent and not share their ideas because of his outwardly aggressive behavior? How many ideas never reached his ears but stayed shuttered in the heads of employees? I did end up securing approval of our new process, as Fred was quite mellow that day. But I will never forget the stories of his awful behavior, and every time I saw him, I found myself unconsciously taking a few steps backward. Sometimes we all need to learn to control our reactions.

You need to know some "brain basics" for two reasons. First, I find it really helps to understand why people act in a particular way. Second, certain differences in how men's and women's brains function cause us to behave differently. The field of neuroscience has only just gotten started looking at these differences, because for a long time, everyone thought a brain was…just a brain. Instead, brains come with many variations, and we've barely begun trying to understand them. The debates rage on in the neuroscience community over whether "female" and "male" brains exist, and I am sure this contention will continue for some time. However, few people argue that men and women behave the same, and ultimately behavior should be our focus, because it's what we experience in the office.

This chapter is intended to be a primer on your brain. I have tried to keep it simple enough and only included some of the basics. In subsequent chapters, we will build on this knowledge as I discuss some of the differences in behavior between people. This foundation will offer you some structure that we will build on throughout the rest of the book.

NEUROPLASTICITY

The adage "you can't teach an old dog new tricks" has been proven completely wrong. Neuroscientists have demonstrated that our brains have significant plasticity and are quite capable of rewiring themselves when offered a stimulus to do so.

Initially, neuroscientists understood that brain development during gestation and infancy was rampant. They believed that as we reached adulthood, the brain became fixed. But new research began to indicate that wasn't true. As told in the book The Mind and the Brain, the neuroscience community did not welcome these new findings with open arms. In fact, much of the early work was met with what one might call complete and vehement denial (just as when Aristotle declared the world was round, most people did not believe him either).[20]

One of the early pioneers in the area of neuroplasticity was Michael Merzenich, now professor emeritus neuroscientist at the University of California, San Francisco. Merzenich was elected into the National Academy of Sciences in May 1999 for his research on brain plasticity. He has

---

20 Schwartz, Jeffrey M. and Begley, Sharon. The Mind and the Brain: Neuroplasticity and the Power of Mental Force. Harper Perennial, 2003.

received numerous other awards and in 2008 was elected to the National Academy Institute of Medicine. He is one of very few who have been elected to more than one of the National Academies. Below is an excerpt from the book The Mind and the Brain (to put part of the quote below in context, you need to know that much of Michael's research was based on studies of monkeys):

"The brain's response to messages from its environment is shaped by its experiences—experiences not only during gestation and infancy, as most neuroscientists were prepared to accept, but by our experience throughout life. The life we live, in other words, shapes the brain we develop," the book reads. "To Michael, the real significance of the findings was what they say about the origins of behavior and mental impairments. 'This machine we call the brain is being modified throughout life,' he mused almost 20 years later. 'The potentiometer for using this for good had been there for years. But it required a different mindset, one that did not view the brain as a machine with fixed parts and defined capacities, but instead as an organ with the capacity to change throughout life. I tried so hard to explain how this would relate to both normal and abnormal behavior. But there were very few takers. Few people grasped the implications.' For a while, it appeared that the monkeys' brains were a lot more adaptable than the research communities."[21]

The tongue-in-cheek humor at the end of this quote is actually driven by what social psychologists call motivated reasoning. All of us have a natural tendency to selectively pick and modify the facts to fit with our own beliefs.

"People are capable of being thoughtful and rational, but our wishes, hopes, fears and motivations often tip the scales to make us more likely to accept something as true if it supports what we want to believe," said Peter Ditto, Ph.D., a social psychologist at the University of California, Irvine.[22]

If we know these types of tendencies exist, we can then use the knowledge to question ourselves and our assumptions when we encounter new information, especially when it contradicts our existing beliefs.

"There are two ways to activate, connect, and grow neural networks," Patt Lind-Kyle writes in her

---

21 Ibid.
22 Weir, Kirsten. "Why We Believe Alternative Facts; How Motivation, Identity and Ideology Combine to Undermine Human Judgement," American Psychological Association, Vol 48, No. 5, May 2017.

book *Heal Your Mind, Rewire Your Brain.*[23] "The first is by repetitive practice like working on a golf swing. The second is through having novel experiences such as taking an adventurous trip or learning a second language — any activity that is not routine. When we are actively engaged in doing something new or that requires practice, the brain changes its structures and functions. When this occurs, the brain's nervous system fires its neural networks in response to this new stimulus. When neurons are activated, their connections to each other change and grow. In addition, supportive cells and blood vessels join them in the activation process. This is the means by which the organization and the volume of brain structures change."

Basically, Patt is saying that your brain is constantly changing based on how you use it. Your neural networks are capable of constant change, and as they change, so does the rest of the brain to support them. So, the next time someone says, "I can't change," you can point this out and say, "It's only a matter of practice or new experiences."

Another message is hidden here: if you want to hire people to drive innovation, who should you look for? I'd say the person with the varied background who has done lots of

---

23 Lind-Kyle, Patt. Heal your Mind, Rewire your Brain. Energy Psychology Press, 2010.

different work, who experiments with the world. That person is more likely to help your teams discover new ideas simply because they like to change things up, which stimulates the mind. They are the person who will bring in different perspectives that kindle innovation and creative ideas.

And, as you will learn later, these folks may be the least likely to be hired by you, particularly if they are different from you. So, be on the lookout for them, even though their differences might make you uncomfortable. Many of these people will be screened out by your hiring team, generally because they don't have the educational background or experience you said you required, so you may need to adjust your requirements to find those who could create breakthrough products for you and drive revenue from places you aren't currently tapping.

MIRROR NEURONS

Mirror neurons were inadvertently discovered in a lab. During an experiment with monkeys, researchers were measuring the monkeys' brain response to pleasure, which they did by monitoring the brain while the monkey ate peanuts. When it was time for a break, the researcher neglected to turn off the equipment. One of the researchers started snacking on the peanuts, and the monkeys watched them eat. Imagine the researchers' shock when they discovered that the monkeys' brains responded in exactly the same manner while they watched the researcher eating the peanuts as they had when eating the peanut themselves. That reaction was caused by mirror neurons.

So, what does this mean for us? Patt Lind-Kyle said it best:[24]

"Remember the old saying 'Learn to appreciate another by walking in their shoes'? Mirror neurons enable us to actually do that. We respond to another's behavior or feeling or 'read another's mind' all the time but are generally not conscious of it. Mirror neurons show us that we are linked on a level of the mind where we can also feel an emotional resonance with people, which connects us. Mirror neurons allow the capacity for opening into empathy toward ourselves and others."

Mirror neurons are a relatively new discovery, and much debate even in the scientific community has been devoted to their purpose and capabilities. Some scientists have asserted that they play a role in our ability to imitate other people's behaviors. They may be part of the tool set we use to learn new skills, by watching others in action. Others have speculated that mirror neurons may aid our ability to understand the actions of others by offering us more of a first-person perspective.[25]

---

24 Ibid.
25 Taylor, John. "Mirror Neurons After a Quarter Century: New light, New Cracks," Science in the News for Harvard Graduate School of the Arts and Sciences, Blog Post, July 25, 2016.

Additionally, some early studies have indicated that there may be sex-based differences with women showing some enhanced empathetic ability over their male counterparts. The debate still rages over whether this disparity is due to the male socialization to limit emotions or whether men and women use different strategies to assess their emotions in response to other people.[26]

YOUR BRAIN

Our brains have three major structures from different evolutionary time periods: the reptilian brain, the limbic system, and the cortex. Our reptilian brain is in the lowest part of the skull; it is the most primitive and oldest part of the brain. Think about this structure as a closed fist. Now wrap your other hand over your closed fist. This top layer is the limbic system. Only mammals have these. If you wrapped a third hand over your second one, that would be the cortex. The cortex and in particular the prefrontal neocortex constitute the latest brain addition in evolutionary terms, emerging only 100,000 years ago.[27]

---

26 Schulte-Rüther, Martin. "Gender Differences in Brain Networks Supporting Empathy," NeuroImage, Vol 42, Issue 1, 1 Aug 2008, pages 393-403.
27 Neubauer, Simon. "Modern Human Brain Organization Emerged Only Recently," Max-Planck-Gesellschaft, Jan 24, 2018.

REPTILIAN BRAIN

The primary parts of the brain and the limbic system are shown in Figure 1 (You can find a color version of this figure along with the latest news and podcasts on the website: www.YouCantFixWhatYouCantSee.com). The reptilian brain consists primarily of the brain stem and the cerebellum, the same components found in reptiles, which together control our bodies' primary functions, such as breathing, heart rate, balance, and movement.[28]

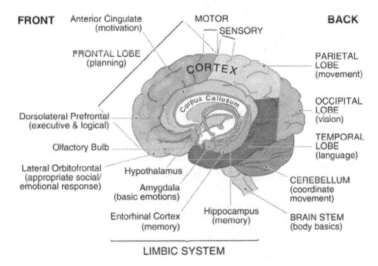

Figure 1: Brain and Limbic System[29]

28 Lind-Kyle, Patt. Heal your Mind, Rewire your Brain. Energy Psychology Press, 2010.
29 Gamon, David. "Your Brain and What It Does", The Brainwaves Center. (Accessed August 2019).

As you might imagine, the reptilian part of our brain is primitive. It controls our fight or flight response and our survival instincts.

I once took a cruise in Alaska on a small boat with about twelve passengers and a naturalist. The trip was designed to allow us to experience as much of the nature around us as possible. Our naturalist would talk about our next adventure and explain what we were going to see, then we would have the experience and talk about it again over dinner.

One day, we went to a deserted island to see the bears. The naturalist, Jim, carefully explained how we should act if we encountered a bear. "Do not run!" he said repeatedly. "Don't turn your back on the bear. Make yourself look large—thrust your arms into the air. Make a lot of noise." I was tingling with excitement, simultaneously so excited that I might see a bear and also terrified, because a lot could go wrong!

We took the motorboat over to the island. It was salmon season, so these huge fish were everywhere, littering the stream. The surrounding area was a rainforest with huge trees and foliage that grew over everything. The sound of the stream gurgling over the rocks was the only noise. I walked in front of the group, eager to see a bear. I wandered up the stream and headed toward the forest, stumbling upon a huge fallen tree that formed a bridge over a smaller stream leading into the lush forest. I thought I would cross over, walking on the tree, and see what was on the other side. I repeated to myself, If you see a bear, don't run; don't turn your back; stay calm; look big.

I had to scramble up onto the tree trunk in order to cross. Just as I got high enough to see over the tree trunk, I saw the bear. It was huge. The bear was planning to use the same log to cross over to the big creek to have a little lunch. We were about thirty feet apart, separated but connected by the fallen tree. The next thing I knew, I found myself running full-tilt back down the riverbank as fast as I could possibly go. I had gone about 300 yards before a tiny voice in my head could finally be heard saying, Don't run! Don't turn your back on a bear. Oops! I took a quick glance behind me, while still running full-tilt, but no bear was on my heels. Phew! Never underestimate the incredible power of your reptilian brain.

Your reptilian brain wants other things as well, including both securing enough food and having shelter. But it also wants to create an organizational structure that makes us feel safe. We know that safety can be found in numbers, and we organize into communities for that reason. The problem with this tendency, which is all too common, is that it can drive an "us vs. them" mentality. Finally, the reptilian brain seeks intimacy with others, in part to ensure the survival of the species, but it also adds energy and togetherness to the balance.

You can think of the parts of the brain as the added layers that make us human. When you look at human evolution, you can see that the brain has added additional layers over a long period of time that differentiate us from other creatures, starting with the reptilian part of the brain we share in common with many creatures.

LIMBIC SYSTEM

The next layer, which sits atop the reptilian layer, is our limbic system. Many mammals have a limbic system. It adds emotions to the reptilian brain: fear, pain, joy, love, but also feelings like wanting to be liked and avoiding pain and discomfort. The limbic system is the part of the brain that learns to repress negative emotions and feelings, which we do by keeping busy with other activities. These repetitive actions wire our brains to continue. Addictions start here when we repeatedly seek pleasure or try to block pain.[30]

The three major parts of the limbic system are the anterior cingulate, amygdala, and hippocampus as shown in Figure 1. The anterior cingulate connects our emotions with our cognitive skills. It is where our self-consciousness originates and allows us to focus our attention, respond with empathy, and regulate our conflicts.[31]

The amygdala monitors incoming signals and is primed to react to ensure your safety. This part of the brain recognizes the saber-toothed tiger (or bear) and sends the danger signal to your reptilian brain. Interestingly, the limbic system does

---

30   Lind-Kyle, Patt. Heal your Mind, Rewire your Brain. Energy Psychology Press, 2010.

31   Ibid.

not mature as we age, which explains why we occasionally see adults in the workplace acting like two-year-old children when their emotional buttons have been pushed.[32] Remember Fred?

The hippocampus is responsible for storing emotional memories after we are about three years old. It captures the emotions and transfers them to long-term memory. Its focus is on survival, including relationship issues related to survival.[33]

CORTEX

The cortex is key to our higher brain function and is the largest structure. It sits on the top of everything that evolved before, as it is the latest addition to our brains. The cortex is divided into two hemispheres connected by a band of nerve fibers called the corpus callosum. These fibers connect the two halves, allowing communication between them. The neocortex is divided into the frontal, parietal, temporal, and occipital lobes, as Figure 1 shows; it is the part of the brain that allows us to think abstractly, develop language, and per-haps most importantly, monitor what's happening around us and decide how we should behave rather than just reacting in a fixed pattern, like our fight or flight response. The neocor-tex holds our personality and our capacity to imagine—here we hold a model of our inner world.[34]

---

32 Ibid
33 Ibid.
34 Ibid.

Our visual, spatial, and imaginative functions are stored in the right hemisphere. The left side houses our logic, linguistic, and linear thinking capabilities. Language, common sense, and judgment take place here.

Interestingly, the right hemisphere is tied directly to our limbic system and the reptilian parts of our brain. For emotions to get to the left, logical side, they must travel from the limbic system to the right hemisphere, then over to the left hemisphere through the corpus callosum. Patt Lind-Kyle summarized the ill-designed impact nicely in her book:[35]

"When our 'head'—our logical abstract side—is cut off from our 'heart' and positive emotions, we can act in a cold-hearted abstract way and not consider the consequences of our actions on others," Patt explains. "In our complex and scary world, it is of great importance to integrate these two functions of head and heart for our future survival."

Our brains are pretty amazing. Scientists are still trying to understand how the parts communicate and how they trigger each other into action, as well as how the neocortex attempts to control a triggered limbic system. There are many powerful triggers we need to watch for:[36]

---

35 Ibid.
36 Heijigers, Harry. "6 Powerful Reptilian Brain hacks to get more Control over your Life", Smart Leadership Hut. (Accessed Sept 2019).

- Threats to safety
- Sex
- Money, power, social status
- Self-image
- Food

Keep in mind that when the triggers above go off, they are setting off primordial forces that are hard to stop. Remember the bear? Well, the naturalist on our cruise has seen many bears and trained himself to not bolt and run away. Stopping these reactions takes some practice, but it can be done. The first step is to recognize that you are being triggered. A brief interval occurs between the triggering event and your body leaping into action, which is when you have the potential to de-escalate your response.

It took me 300 yards before the rational part of my brain was able to break through with the message, Do not run! With practice, you can learn to temper your innate responses.

A great example of this phenomenon is the fear of public speaking. Many people have conquered their fear, through training, coaching, and programs like Toastmasters. These programs don't just teach you skills; they also give you lots of opportunity to practice. Repetitive practice is what builds neural networks in your brain to give you a more reliable response. You can take charge of your reptilian brain, but it may take some practice.

You must be very careful that the actions you take don't trigger other people's reptilian brains. The list above represents some of the most powerful triggers. You must identify the triggers that set you off and make you act in a way you may later regret.

My mom was a very practical person. Often, when we were shopping, I would find something I "just had to have." She would say, "Is this something you will really wear?" Of course, I would say, "Yes!" She knew better, though. What she knew was that my social status and self-image triggers had been activated and she found a way to tame them. "Okay," she would say, "we can put it on hold and if tomorrow you really still think you need it, we can come back and buy it." More than 90 percent of those items we did not go back and get. About half the time, I never even remembered the next day the item that was singing so sweetly to me the day before.

Sales people everywhere press customers to make a decision now, while our brains are triggered with "want." Just delaying our decisions can do a world of good for us when our brains are triggered, and we think we have to act immediately.

***

Neuroscience is opening up a whole new world of revelations about how our brains work. Neuroplasticity tells us that we indeed can learn new tricks through a combination of repetition or new experiences. Our mirror neurons can help us experience other people's feelings and engage our empathy.

Our brain is a complex organ with many components that work together to allow us to get along in the world. It has many shortcuts and secret decoders that, from an evolutionary perspective, have served us well. However, because many of these operate in the background and are not conscious to us, we find it easy to keep reacting the same way because of these scripts.

Now that you know about this phenomenon, your job is to start watching your reactions. Ask yourself, Is that the way I want to show up in the world? If you desire a different response, start working on programming it into your brain. You can use repetition and new experiences to build new neural networks. And, now that you understand some of the primordial brain triggers, you can begin monitoring your own reactions. Sometimes you may want to decide that you wish to have a different response and begin to program that into your brain.

Want some practice? Pick a reaction you have that you'd like to change. For some, maybe you want to stop being triggered when you are driving, perhaps some things your kids do trigger you (they are quite adept at this), or perhaps you have triggers around food. Pick one reaction you would like to change in yourself and start working on it. It may take a couple of weeks of practice, but you can change your reaction through repetition.

CHAPTER 4

OUR DIFFERENCES: INTRODUCTION

A human being is a part of the whole, called by us universe, a part limited in time and space. He experiences himself, his thoughts and feelings as something separated from the rest, a kind of optical delusion of his consciousness. This delusion is a kind of prison for us, restricting us to our personal desires and to affection for a few persons nearest to us. Our task must be to free ourselves from this prison by widening our circle of compassion to embrace all living creatures and the whole of nature in its beauty.

—ALBERT EINSTEIN

The one fact scientists can all agree on is that all brains are different. The basic components and functions of the brain were discussed in chapter three. In this chapter, I will focus on differences in people's brains and behaviors. How our behaviors are interpreted largely depends on who is doing the interpreting, as you will see. I will preface this section with the caution that significant disagreement still exists among scientists about these differences and the cause of perceived differences. However, mounting evidence both from the neuroscientists and the psychologists suggests that men and women function differently. We can all gain some insight from understanding some of these basic differences and how they may manifest themselves in our behavior.

In a 2014 study, scientists discovered some dramatic sex differences in the wiring of men's and women's brains.[37] This study examined brains of 949 people using MRI scanning. The researchers then parceled the brain into ninety-five regions and created structural connectomes shown in Figure 2 based on the connection probability between the regions derived from the composite MRI data. Connectomes are visual representations of the interconnected network of neurons in your brain. These images are captured

---

37 Ingalhalikar, Madhura and Smith, Alex, and Parker, Drew, Satterthwaite, Theodore D. and Elliott, Mark A and Ruparel, Kosha, and Hakonarson, Hakon and Gur, Raquel E. and Gur, Ruben C. and Verma, Ragini. Proceedings of the National Academy of Sciences of the USA, January 14, 2014 111 (2) 823-828.

based on the normal passage or diffusion of water through the nerve fibers. The results are rather dramatic.

Many men's preferential patterns represent a "perceive then act" sequence of brain function as indicated by the front-to-rear activity in their brains in the top half of Figure 2. Women's patterns (shown in the bottom half of Figure 2) exhibit more lateral connectivity between the two hemispheres representing a balancing of the analytical and intuitive processes (You will find a color version of this picture and other tantalizing tidbits on the website: www.YouCantFixWhatYouCantSee.com). We all think differently. But long before the scientists had been able to "see" this phenomenon, almost any couple who has had a long-term relationship could have told you this was true, while providing ample graphic and often humorous examples from their own relationships.

Let's use a simple example to clarify what we are seeing. Imagine you are called to an emergency meeting with a few other colleagues. In the meeting, one of your technicians gets on the phone and is reporting back on some rather strange, never-before-seen data that your equipment is generating. The technician is calling in because he has never experienced such results and is at a loss as to what action he should take. One of the engineers in the room starts asking some questions about the equipment, and he finally says, "Okay, I think we should replace Widget 1. I'll go get one from the warehouse and overnight it to you." This response is a classic perceive then act sequence.

Just as the first engineer gets up to go get the part, another engineer pipes up, and she says, "Wait a minute. Didn't this just get installed on their new prototype line? Maybe we should verify that the right signals are being sent to the equipment. You know, it could also be Widget 2, or perhaps one of the connectors is shorting out." She has just brought in new information: the equipment is installed on a prototype at the customer's facility, meaning the client is still developing the line and perhaps didn't have everything connected properly. It may not even be your equipment; perhaps it's really on the client's side. The second engineer may have arrived at this conclusion through intuition and analysis based on the fact that no one has seen the data look like that and the customer is creating a new process. The two engineers talk some more and agree that they should overnight several parts out and the technician should perform a couple of tests on the client's signals being fed into your machine. In this example, both engineers were in the room and heard the same information but came to different conclusions. This case also illustrates the point that having both types of thinking in the room may allow you to come up with a more robust solution.

Our brains are wired a bit differently. These differences in wiring, along with many other differences, result in amazing variation in how we perceive, process information, and what we value as important.

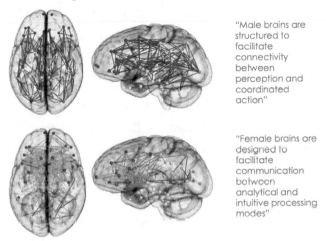

"Male brains are structured to facilitate connectivity between perception and coordinated action"

"Female brains are designed to facilitate communication between analytical and intuitive processing modes"

Figure 2: Brain Connectivity in Men's and Women's Brains[38]

DICHOTOMIES

Before we begin to look at our differences, I want to clarify some context. We are all different; that's what makes each of us unique. We are a complex mix of our genes, cultural upbringing, and life experiences. Throughout this book, I will talk about the traits or tendencies of people. First, you must understand that many of our behaviors represent a dichotomy, and each of us can find ourselves anywhere along the spectrum for any given trait, while for another

---

38 Ibid.

trait, you may find you are in a very different spot along that particular dichotomy.

Edward Hall and Geert Hofstede developed a lot of research around high – and low-context cultures. Low-context cultures are rather individualistic, like the United States, whereas high-context cultures like Japan are communal or community-focused. Context can be thought of as a high-level view of cultural differences. The styles of these cultures can be quite different, and these differences can make it difficult to navigate. Imagine people who are working at a startup company, with only a few people who wear many hats: the context will be low, as they have not had time to build up a set of protocols or processes and procedures on how work gets done. Compare that to what goes on in a big Fortune 500 Company, with rules, procedures, job descriptions. It has a much higher context culture. Now, when a Fortune 500 company buys a startup company, the two organizations end up with a clash of contexts. If this mixture is not managed well, the employees from the startup may all bail out as they feel the "rules" are overwhelming. Likewise, the Fortune 500 employees may describe the startup employees as undisciplined and out of control because they cannot seem to follow the rules of the "mothership."

Understanding that people can be very different from one another, just as cultures are, drove me to create a similar model as Hall & Hofstede, focusing on individuals' tendencies instead of cultural ones.

Throughout this book, I will present several dichotomies that will help explain people's behaviors and put them in some context. To help you build a mental framework you can easily use, I will be labeling each of the dichotomies with a common scale ranging from an independent to a community orientation as shown in Figure 3. Some people would want to label these tendencies as more characteristic of men or women. However, I have found that for any given dichotomy, a man or woman can actually be anywhere along the continuum. Some of the dichotomies we'll explore in the next chapter include convergent vs. divergent thinking and divide & conquer vs. share & build.

Figure 3: Independent – vs Community-Minded Dichotomy

I, for example, find that I possess some very distinctive "independent" traits in some areas, which may be a result of working in technology for many years. They may also be a result of being raised by an independent and strong-willed mother. Where these characteristics came from is nowhere near as important as my understanding of where I am on that spectrum in relation to other people, and the recognition that others may be in a very different place. At the same time, I've found that being in one place with a given dichotomy does not mean you will be in the same relative position for a different dichotomy. So, while I am very much on the independent side with one set of characteristics, I may be very much aligned with the community side on a different trait. With this knowledge, I can choose to interpret what I perceive as differences in a more knowledgeable light, one that helps open the door to new understanding.

The other reason for creating these dichotomies is to offer a common language that can be taken into the workplace to start communications on a much deeper level than what typically takes place today. One of the hallmarks of a strong culture is that it has created a common language around what it values. Many companies have not yet expanded their cultural definition to include discussion around the dichotomies that will be presented here. I hope these new definitions will offer us a choice of language to facilitate more meaningful conversations about our differences.

Many articles and books over the years have described differences between men and women, and some have gone so far to conclude that one side is "correct" and the other "wrong." Quite a bit of blame and shame has been cast about which never seems to be very productive. Conversations that offer us the possibility to move away from the blame and shame, give us the opportunity to have a deeper level of conversation about our differences. This allows us to explore our differences, understand them, appreciate them, and even leverage them to make our workplaces more engaging.

Finally, as you go through the next three chapters, keep in mind that no "right" position exists on any of the dichotomies. They simply represent different perspectives. Neither is right or wrong. In fact, as you will see, what may be most important is having people in several different places, representing different viewpoints. This diversity of thought will yield the best results in terms of better decision making, strategy development, innovation, and employee engagement.

The other critical factor is that you develop the capacity within your organization to openly discuss these differences. When it becomes the norm to discuss these dichotomies, people will find that they are able to transcend the labels we frequently use and actually arrive at a deeper understanding of where people are coming from. It allows us to get to the deeper "why." Once you actually take the time to understand other people's positions, you understand the assumptions they are making and can discuss them to determine if that person is really the best one to handle a given situation.

INTENTION

What I have frequently seen is that the sexes misinterpret the manifestation of behavior, adding a component of intent by the other person that may or may not actually be there. In other words, we each interpret other people's behavior in accordance with our own lens of perception, then may interpret the other person's intent according to our own lens.

Many assumptions contribute to this process that we are frequently unaware we are making. We may need to first "see" the assumptions we employ and do some additional validation before reaching a conclusion.

One of my bosses held a weekly one-on-one meeting with me. I would sit at his table and he would sit at his desk where his computer was located. During the first few of these meetings, we would discuss the programs I was creating. However, he would frequently look at his computer screen and sometimes proceed to answer an email or text while I was talking with him. This behavior went on for a few weeks, and I began to get rather irritated, so I began to stop talking when he was focused on his computer or phone. When he realized I was silent, he said: "Karen, I'm very good at multitasking. You can keep talking; I just need to respond to this email," at which point I replied, "Actually, you are not good at multitasking. You are choosing to do something else during the time we have set aside to collaborate. This is very frustrating to me."

Now, I could have taken his actions personally and been thinking, He doesn't care about what I am working on, or He doesn't want to listen to me, or Other projects are more important to him. All of these thoughts could lead me to the conclusion that he was a bad boss who didn't care in general about his employees or specifically about me. However, none of that was true.

He really thought he was good at multitasking and that his actions were not adversely affecting our conversations. He thought he was being efficient. As soon as I pointed out that it wasn't true for me, he got up from his desk and came over to the table where I sat, away from both his computer and phone. Even better was the fact that, for all subsequent meetings, he immediately joined me at his table for our discussions.

We all must be careful about ascribing malicious intent to other people's actions. Before we assume intent, we should try to validate it. The simple act of doing this forces us to consider what their intent was and if it was valid, and the confirmation of the validity may often reveal other factors that have been unspoken but could prove useful to you.

Once, I thought that I was being unfairly called out in a meeting. I asked the person after the meeting what they meant by their remark. They told me that it was actually a message for another person in the room, but I happened to be the one who brought up the subject that made him remember he wanted to make that point. It really had nothing to do with me. But I also wonder if the intended recipient got the message, since the comment was directed at me.

OUR DIFFERENCES

I have organized the next three chapters into three loose categories of differences: processing, perception, and value. These categories were derived from observed behavior differences between people. They are visually depicted in Figure 4 in the form of a telescope, because our differences form a lens through which we view the world. Different people may be in the same room with us but see the situation completely differently because of their lens. Since we are both in the same room, we think we experienced the same thing, but subsequent conversations may make us wonder if we were in different rooms or if it's really different, maybe even if we were on different planets.

The other image in Figure 4 is your secret decoder, depicted by a triangle. I include this representation to remind each of us that we have our own version of how we believe things work. One of our goals as we learn more about our differences is to add additional dimensions to our secret decoders to help us understand that others see things a bit differently. We will add more to this model in the last chapter.

Figure 4: Our Differences: Processing, Perception, and Value

Processing includes how we process information—how we think—and how we prefer to work. Perception is how we perceive information and others' behavior. Value focuses on what we each value and consider important. I do not believe these three categories are independent of each other; in fact, I believe much overlap exists. I simply wanted to break down the dichotomies into smaller and similar clusters that would make them easier to think about, understand, and explore.

I have found that understanding we exhibit some distinct behavior differences allows us to interpret these differences in a new light as we are forced to look through a different perception lens. This exercise forces people to think about and identify the assumptions they are making and offers the opportunity for validation, a step we frequently miss. This validation can keep us from misinterpreting what we are seeing and driving us to take a direction that may be counter to the one leading us out of the chasm of misunderstanding and blame into an area of deeper understanding.

CHAPTER 5

OUR DIFFERENCES: PROCESSING

The world as we have created it is a process of our thinking. It cannot be changed without changing our thinking.

—ALBERT EINSTEIN

PROCESSING

In the previous chapter, we looked at how men's and women's brains are wired differently. So, what does this biology mean in our everyday lives?

Let's take a look at an example to see how it shows up.

Imagine your boss walks into your office and says, "I think we've identified a problem, and I want you to take a look at it and figure out how to approach it."

If you are on the independent-minded side of the dichotomy (like many men), you tend to want to sit down and think about it on your own first. You would mull it over, all the while focusing in deeper to try and understand the problem. You would start to identify causes and immediately discard those that don't fit. You would sort through the facts you know about the situation and use this information to narrow the problem down as you progress in your thinking. After you'd gone through this process, you would relate your findings back to your boss.

If you are a community-minded person (like many women), you would first get four or five other knowledgeable people involved, to solicit their opinions and talk about: What is the problem? When did it show up? How long has it persisted? Did we change anything recently? You'd spend a lot of time on this phase until you felt you understood the problem. Many "what if" questions would be asked during this process. You probably wouldn't complete this evaluation in one sitting. In fact, you might decide to let it "rest" for a while and start working on it again the next day, knowing that frequently, this approach results in new insights and more questions to answer, after you've had a chance to cogitate on it awhile.

Now, put these two styles together in the workplace. The independent-minded would like to go off and think about the problem first; the community-minded would want to talk about it first. Here's your first clash. The community-minded want to explore a lot of possibilities—not weeding them out, but coming up with an infinitely long list. The independent-minded keep taking items off the list, while the community-minded keep adding possibilities that may be seemingly more and more far-fetched to the independent-minded. This difference marks the second conflict. At the end of the day, the community-minded want to think about it, and the independent-minded just want a conclusion to take back to the boss. These two styles seem diametrically opposed, leaving everyone frustrated. Both parties feel their approach is right, and surely the other person is taking an approach that will not work. Both are thinking, What are you doing? of the other person.

Have you had this experience at work?

Both people are working in the style they understand. The piece neither person may get is that the other person's style is not wrong, flawed, or destined to fail. Each person is doing what works for them based on the way their brain is wired. In fact, the combination of the two styles will most likely offer the best result, if they can work together long enough to appreciate their differences.

Knowing these processing differences can help you design how you approach the work a little differently to accommodate the differences. For example, you might have an initial meeting to simply introduce the problem to the team, then schedule a meeting for the next day to talk about different approaches. This method allows the independent-minded people time to ponder the problem on their own. Likewise, it permits those who are community-minded time to discuss the problem with others, which is what they need to formulate their thoughts on the situation. Both parties can then fully participate in the meeting the following day, prepared to discuss the appropriate approach.

This difference shows up prominently in the work of Barbara Annis and Keith Merron. In their book Gender Intelligence,[39] they describe the tendencies that men and women have when making decisions, as shown in Table 1. Barbara says women (who are primarily community-minded) tend to go deep and broad and think problems through more fully, while men (primarily independent-minded) lean toward being fast and focused in decision-making. You may note that this ties in very well with the brain differences discussed in the previous chapter. Facts drive decisions for the independent-minded, while the community-minded also rely on intuition.

The independent-minded think in a linear or stepwise manner and keep their focus on the end goal, while the

---

39 Annis, Barbara and Merron, Keith. Gender Intelligence; Breakthrough Strategies for Increasing Diversity and Improving Your Bottom Line. HarperBusiness, 2014.

community-minded use more multidimensional thinking and consider the consequences of their decision, which alters their perceptions of the factors that should be considered while making decisions.

Women's Tendencies	Men's Tendencies
Think through more fully	Think and act quickly
Intuitive	Fact-based
Multi-dimensional thinking	Stepwise thinking
Consider the consequences	Focus on the goal

Table 1: Women's and Men's Tendencies in Decision-Making[40]

As you can see from all these differences, quite a few areas seem to foreshadow conflict. I have often been in a meeting where a community-minded person brings up a question and it is either ignored by the independent-minded or met with a comment like "What does that have to do with this topic?" The community-minded person knows how they arrived at this consideration but neglects to share that information, tailoring to the independent-minded's need to be focused and fast. The independent-minded have no clue how the question the community-minded brought up relates to the topic at hand, and so they dismiss the information as irrelevant or extraneous. The community-minded, feeling ignored and not valued, may now stop attempting to contribute, leaving a critical knowledge gap in the conversation.

---

40 Ibid.

Here's an example:

Let's say you are a local Indiana company that creates recipes and cookbooks. Suddenly, you start getting complaints from consumers that their cakes baked from your recipes are all gooey inside. You are in a meeting brainstorming what could possibly be going wrong. You discuss ingredients, oven temperatures, and a whole host of other factors, but you haven't quite figured out what is happening. Then someone asks where the complaints originated. Everyone in the room looks at that person and says, "What difference does that make?" effectively killing the question off. The meeting concludes with the assumption that consumers are just not following the recipe.

Now, let's replay the meeting with a different twist that allows you to leverage the diversity in the room. When someone asks, "Where did the complaints originate?" the response is "Let's see if we know." After checking, they discover that at least one customer was from Colorado. Someone asks, "How did our cookbooks get to Colorado?" Another pipes up and says, "Oh yes, a small bookstore chain there ordered a couple of boxes of books. Oh, we've never shipped our cookbooks out of state before." Bingo! The elevation difference between Colorado and Indiana is huge. And the solution becomes clear: you need to add high-elevation cooking instructions and adjust the ingredients due to the lower air pressure at higher elevations.

A very different outcome than the conclusion that customers weren't following the recipe.

And, after the company adds the recipe modifications, its interstate business continues to grow.

***

Why do we think so differently?

Our brains are wired a bit differently, as we learned in chapter four. And we understand that neuroplasticity allows the brain to constantly rewire itself, driven by the activities we participate in. So how our brain is wired now may not be how it is wired next year or five years from now.

There are also other differences in the structures of men's and women's brains. The corpus callosum is the bundle of nerve fibers connecting the left and right hemispheres of the brain. The right hemisphere is where creative thought and imagination and intuition take place. It is directly connected to the limbic system, which is where our emotions originate. For emotions to get over to the left hemisphere, they have to travel from the limbic system into the right hemisphere and then through the corpus callosum over to the left hemisphere. Once in the left hemisphere, emotions can get factored into decisions, as this side of the brain is responsible for our logic and judgment. Women's corpus callosums are physically larger than men's.

Frank Browning in his book The Fate of Gender wrote that:[41]

---

41   Browning, Frank. The Fate of Gender; Nature, Nurture, and the Human Future. Bloomsbury USA, 2016.

"There is mounting evidence that women enjoy greater translateral access across the corpus callosum between left and right hemispheres than do men: Men's mental activity, remember, tends to be concentrated, sometimes isolated, on the so-called cognitive side while women, on average, access both right and left hemispheres more readily. For some researchers and their activist followers, that cerebral fluidity helps explain women's supposed richer access to intuition and creative insight, which one might suppose would enhance their advantage over men in both the sciences and the arts. Alas, few societies anywhere in the world seem yet to have profited from that advantage, suggesting that socially created gender regimes consistently trump innate 'sex' differences. Perhaps women's greater success at university will one day change that."

Many factors drive these differences, in the brain, our DNA, and our experiences. Dr. Jennifer Ashton offered these brain differences along with her "thinkers and linkers" nomenclature in The Fate of Gender:[42]

"Vast functional differences between women's and men's brains—from the greater mass and weight

_____

42   Ibid.

of grey matter in male brains to the slightly greater amount of white matter in female brains, as well as citing autopsy based evidence that female brains have more trans-lateral 'neuro-wiring' than male's brains in the corpus callosum tying together the right and left hemispheres. These measurable volumes and linkages help explain how and why men excel at 'processing information' while women excel at connecting or linking the 'processing centers' within the brain. Women are 'linkers,' men are 'thinkers.' ... Women are more adept at multifunctional thinking and maintaining interpersonal connections while men triumph at singularly focused, concentrated thinking."

Somehow, women seem to be able to factor more emotional content into their thinking. Is that driven by how our brains are wired? Or by the fact that men are socialized from a very young age to minimize emotions? The years of emotional suppression may have diminished men's capacity to actually feel their emotions. I contend that maybe it doesn't matter how: it may be enough for us to understand that this point is where we are now.

Diane Halpern at the Claremont Colleges group wrote:[43]

---

43   Ibid.

"The question is not if either female and male brains are similar or different, because they are both. The questions we need to answer are: How can we understand the ways in which we are similar and different? And how can we use that knowledge to help everyone achieve their fullest potential?"

***

Several other categories lie along a dichotomy that we can consider in looking at the differences in the behavior of people. Taking the information and examples above, we can describe several more of these continuums. As we review these continuums, keep in mind that I will be describing the two extremes. Most of us will find we aren't on one end or the other, but somewhere in the middle.

As you read these, consider a recent situation and think about what behaviors you exhibited. Where were you along the dichotomy? If you recall a few situations, you may find that under different circumstances you behave differently. Our behaviors can be very situational, and our brains dynamically decide how we are going to be. This phenomenon typically happens unconsciously, without our knowledge.

One of the keys to being able to leverage diversity is to first become aware of what point on a given dichotomy you naturally gravitate toward. Then, as you become aware you can bring your choices into the realm of conscious decisions. You can move from:

"Where am I?" to "Where do I want to be?"

INDEPENDENT VS. COLLABORATIVE THINKING

First, let's take a look at how we prefer to work and process information. The independent-minded lean toward, expectedly, independent thinking; they need to prioritize and identify their own path to a solution when they are making a decision or solving a problem. To do so, their preferred method of working is by themselves, as illustrated in the first example in this chapter. The independent-minded may get frustrated if they are forced into a collaborative environment before they've had a chance to think it through alone first. This method of thinking may be the fastest and is certainly less resource-intensive than collaborative thinking. The dichotomy is shown in Figure 5.

Independent ⟵——————⟶ Collaborative

Figure 5: Independent vs. Collaborative Thinking

The community-minded prefer to work in a more collaborative environment. They use the collaboration to identify things like: What factors should be considered? Who are the stakeholders? Who might be impacted by this decision? What are the long-term implications? Community thinkers prefer this collaborative style and use their discussions to build context around the problem. Since more people are involved, this approach can require significantly more resources.

CONVERGENT VS. DIVERGENT THINKING

A second category is how we think. There are convergent and divergent thinkers. The thinking processed are depicted in Figure 6.

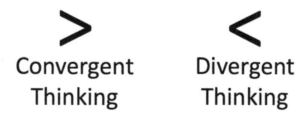

Figure 6: Convergent vs. Divergent Thinking

The independent-minded lean toward convergent thinking as they focus in and try to get to the heart of the problem. With convergent thinking, your focus is on narrowing down possibilities. Eliminating those that don't fit. Reducing the number and combination of variables. You get rid of variables that you feel don't need to be considered immediately. This type of thinking can often get you to a result faster, as it's easier to eliminate items than to add them.

On the opposite end of the spectrum, you have divergent thinking. The community-minded tend to lean toward the divergent side. They expand the context of items that should be considered when tackling a problem. Here, you would consider more factors, look beyond the surface, and try to identify secondary considerations and the factors associated with those considerations. You might ask yourself or your team more questions to stimulate your thinking, like "What would be the consequences if we...?" and from that generate more factors to be considered. The divergent thinking process is likely to take more time. Figure 7 shows the dichotomy for this characteristic.

Figure 7: Convergent vs. Divergent Thinking

So, which one of these thinking styles do you lean toward? Which one is better?

Often, the best results come when you use a combination of these two, although again it may be highly dependent on the situation at hand.

For example, when problem-solving, you might want to start off with more divergent thinking to bring in a wide realm of possibilities and identify all the factors you should take into consideration. Then move toward convergent thinking, narrowing down or eliminating ones you don't need to think about. Timing should also be a consideration. In a crisis, you may need to go for speed initially. But as your focus shifts from the immediate to the longer run, adding in some divergent thinking may get you to a more robust long-term solution.

Next time you are in a brainstorming meeting, try to figure out who leans on convergent thinking and who prefers divergent. Speak up and ask, "Should we be using convergent thinking here or would our session produce better results if we used a little divergent thinking first?" Often, most people are unaware of their own preference until someone voices what is happening. Remember it's a choice, but most people don't realize they even have one to make. You can be the catalyst to ask, "What method might give us the best outcome?"

INFORMATION: BARTERING VS. SHARING

In our world, information has been at the heart of knowledge (at least in the pre-digital era). How knowledge is used by people is interesting. The community-minded tend to share knowledge and will frequently offer up information that they feel may help another person in a given situation.

The independent-minded use information as a form of currency. They barter the information, seldom offering it up spontaneously. You have to ask them for it. Many people in high-level positions in companies actively barter information as if it were power. Who gets access to the new organization chart before it is announced? Who has access to information about clients and who has to dig for it? Who volunteers information and who do you have to ask (sometimes repeatedly) to pry information from them? The information dichotomy is shown in Figure 8.

Figure 8: Information Bartering vs. Sharing

It's as if the community-minded take a moment to think, What information do I have that this person can benefit from? The independent-minded, when offered this type of information, often respond with "Why are you telling me this?"

What's worse is if, when offered this information, the independent-minded get upset and a bit insulted, then say, "I don't need your help. I can do this myself." (I will talk a bit more about this in the next chapter, as it is tied to status and independence.) Then the community minded person will stomp off, muttering, "I was just trying to help!"

This example shows how it goes wrong. The interaction could go a lot better if people were aware of their own and others' tendencies. Once you understand someone's preference, you can leverage it. Let's say you are a sharer and the person you want to get information to is a barterer. They like to barter, so use this knowledge. You have information you think would be valuable to them, but you don't want to trigger that defensive reaction, so don't just offer them the information; ask for something you need in return—remember, they prefer to barter!

The community-minded may have a tendency to spend too much time sharing information, which might come in the form of gossip or sharing personal information. The independent-minded may easily get frustrated by what appears to be non-work-related chitchat.

CONTROL VS. EMPOWERMENT

Because independent – and community-minded people think differently, they approach power differently as well. The independent-minded are well-versed in the command-and-control mentality that started in the military and gained favor during the industrial era. Under this regime, the strategy is set at the top of the organization and directions (or orders) are issued that, if carried out properly, will result in proper execution of the strategy. One of the hallmarks of this style is that your job is to carry out the orders, not question them. It is clear, concise, efficient, and effective.

The community-minded lean toward a different mentality, which, I admit, can drive the independent-minded a bit nuts, but it's how the community-minded like to work. It's like they are thinking, I will take the time to lay out what we need to accomplish and even to spell out some of the outcomes that are necessary. Once I do this, you should have all the information you need to decide what is the best way of constructing a solution for the problem at hand. As the knowledge era descends upon us, I expect this approach will gain more favor as it is more attuned with the nature of knowledge work. Figure 9 depicts the control vs. empowerment dichotomy.

Figure 9: Control vs. Empowerment

So, how do you work across these two styles?

Let's say you thrive on empowerment but are working with a boss who prefers to exert more control. First, take a minute to chat with them about your style and offer a suggestion of how they can get the best results from you. Your conversation with your command-and-control boss might go something like this:

"I do my best work when I have some autonomy in figuring out how to accomplish my goals. It really helps me if you can explain 'what' you want to accomplish and then let me figure out how to go about it. I especially would like it if you would let me know about any special requirements or considerations, like 'make sure to include someone from this group since I already mentioned this to their boss and she wants her group involved.' I can also formulate my plan and then run it by you, if need be, to make sure I have all the bases covered."

Recognize that releasing this level of control may be daunting for people who prefer command and control, hence the offer to review your plan before you get started. You may need to add in other touch points to make your boss more comfortable. The issue here is that if they feel like they are losing control, you will need to give them assurance along the way. Then, after your project is complete, make sure you go back and ask them how this process went for them. You can factor their feedback into the next project, and over time they will become much more comfortable giving you more autonomy.

I have one added tip for gaining more empowerment. The command-and-control boss always wants to be in control. Their worst fear is having something blow up in their face and not knowing enough about what has transpired to even answer a question from their superiors. Do not let this happen, ever! As soon as you even think something is amiss, you need to be in your boss's office giving them an update.

I trained my project managers to proceed this way, and it works wonderfully.

About 5 a.m. one morning, I got a call from one of my project managers. He told me to put a pot of coffee on and wait about thirty minutes for a call from his client, who was royally pissed off. The project manager updated me on the project, let me know what had caused the client to flip out, and informed me about several other factors I needed to know, including some things he needed to get from the client. When the client called me, I understood exactly where the project was and what the issues were. I also had a pocketful of factors I knew were important for this client and a few things we needed in order to ultimately make the project a success. We ended up having a great chat: I was able to smooth the ruffled feathers out, actually building our relationship further, and come to an agreement about how to proceed that worked in both of our favors. I could only accomplish this feat, however, because my project manager called me first with the heads-up.

Over the years, I have often walked into my boss's office and let them know potential problems were brewing that they needed to be aware of. Perhaps only 25 percent of the time they actually got a subsequent call, but keeping my boss in the loop built a tremendous amount of trust between us that often resulted in me getting even more autonomy. I had their back, and they knew it.

CREDIT: TAKING VS. GIVING

The community-minded like to give credit, and the independent-minded prefer to take it. When the community-minded discuss their accomplishments, it comes out like: "My team accomplished this." They phrase it that way because, for them, acknowledging that the team was key in the accomplishment is crucial. It is not adequate for the community-minded to simply solve a problem. Their team must be along for the ride and fully brought in. This thinking will ensure the participation of all members for the next project.

For the independent-minded, it's the "I" pronoun. This tendency could happen for a number of reasons, but a lot of it may derive from the relational nature of the community-minded and the independent nature of independent-minded. Additionally, the independent-minded are generally focused first on their own status, rather than the status of their team (this status component will be discussed in more detail in the next chapter). Figure 10 depicts the credit dichotomy.

Figure 10: Taking vs. Giving Credit

Giving credit and sharing it with others is important. But how do you get people to do it? Some people use what is called an amplification strategy. It goes like this: Someone brings up an idea in a meeting and it does not get recognized initially. You think it's a good idea, then someone else re-suggests it as if it were their own. At this point, you chime in and say, "Sally just brought that up a few minutes ago; let's have her add to what you just said, since she initially brought it up."

Unfortunately, some people are serial credit stealers. A good strategy for rectifying this situation is to recruit a couple of people and use the amplification approach discussed above consistently in meetings. In this case, it is better to have someone else gently reframe where the idea originated. It also sends a subtle message to the credit thief that you give credit where credit is due.

Some recent studies have examined this phenomenon from a slightly different perspective. In one particular study, researchers looked at people who speak up in meetings specifically about how to improve their teams. They studied how such actions affected the team's perception of those people's leadership capabilities. Speaking up in meetings implies that you know what you are talking about and have the team's well-being in mind. The study then looked at the question of: when the team needs a new leader, who is more likely to be nominated by the team to serve in that role?[44]

---

44 University of Delaware. "Women get less credit than men in the workplace." ScienceDaily. ScienceDaily, 13 December 2017.

Their findings are quite surprising. Men, who speak up more often than two-thirds of their teammates, are voted to be the number-two candidate to lead the team. Women, on the other side, who speak up the same amount, are voted to be the number-eight candidate to lead the team. So, men who speak up quite a lot are seen as leadership material, while women who speak up just as much as the men are not ranked very high as leadership material by the team itself. Unfortunately, I believe this result shows the unconscious bias many have regarding women, leadership, and being outspoken. What is good for the goose is not good for the gander (this topic will be discussed more in the next chapter as well).

They did a subsequent study which resulted in some interesting findings:

"We find that men are given more credit than women even when saying exactly the same thing." – Kyle Emich, assistant professor of management at the University of Delaware.

Perhaps the most interesting part of the research is how people react to these statistics. Kyle says women are not shocked, but men are mostly oblivious. "This is because [men] do not need to consider their gender in most organizational contexts, thus their unconscious biases remain just that, unconscious," he explains.

Now, at your next meeting, try observing who is speaking up and who is getting credit (or taking credit) for ideas. When you start to see a disparity, speak up. It matters.

DIVIDE & CONQUER VS. SHARE & BUILD

Another approach that the independent-minded lean toward is the divide-and-conquer method for work. Their thought process works as such: "Divide all the work up; we'll each do these parts, then we can pull them back together in the end." This tactic allows people to work independently on their part of the solution and is an efficient method coming out of the industrial era. You just need to spend a little time designing the interfaces between the parts up front and merging the pieces together at the end.

The community-minded prefer a different method: they gather together and discuss what they are planning, allowing all to contribute to the overall design. They discuss how it will go together and what the desired outcomes are. The old-fashioned quilting bee has a very similar model. Everyone contributes to all parts; they work together during the design, construction, and finishing stage. Now, don't get me wrong: everyone doesn't work on everything. In fact, people who are really good in a particular area may focus on the part where they excel, but they should be a participant in the planning discussions, so they know how their part fits into the larger whole. Because of this knowledge, they know that if they are going to shift the way they want to implement their part, they will need to let people with adjacent work know so everyone ends up with the same schema. That way, when they combine it all together, it actually fits. The dichotomy for this component is shown in Figure 11.

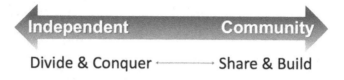

Independent ◄————————► Community

Divide & Conquer ·————————· Share & Build

Figure 11: Divide & Conquer vs. Share & Build

Either of these methods works; the question you need to answer is which works better for the project you are trying to deliver.

I went to work for a company and just four weeks after I started, it flipped the switch on a brand-new enterprise resource planning (ERP) system for managing production schedules, part-ordering, and inventory. What's more, this was a pilot system that was supposed to be fine-tuned by our division and then used as the model for the entire company. Let's just say that the implementation did not go very well. Maybe I am being too generous: it was actually an unmitigated disaster.

It took a couple of weeks for us to realize that the system was automatically reordering all parts not in stock (on a daily basis) regardless of whether they had been previously ordered. The warehouse overflowed and became completely dysfunctional as boxes of parts kept arriving one wave after another, until the building was completely full and boxes were stacked in the hallways and everywhere in our offices. No one could find a thing.

About four weeks after the system went live, I sat down to talk to one of the developers. Over a cup of coffee, I explained how we worked with our customers. As I talked, the color drained out of the developer's face and he started to sweat. I honestly thought something was really wrong with him and I asked as much. His reply was: "If what you're telling me is true, then this system will never work for you—we'll have to completely redesign it."

Somewhere along the way, either when they broke apart the project into its parts or when they started pulling the pieces back together, some key components, like how we actually worked with our customers, got lost in the shuffle. The company was still redesigning the system when I left five months later, and full implementation across the company was pushed out by more than a year. Six years later, the company, once a twice Malcolm Baldrige Quality Award winner, was purchased by one of its competitors.

When you are deciding how to accomplish large projects, the level of integration needed and the potential for iterations that change the scope should be taken into consideration. Heavy integration and a high potential for changes should lead you toward a share-and-build approach. This tactic is similar to agile planning for software where, as iterations occur, the team is brought together to figure out how to deal with a dynamically changing situation. The divide-and-conquer approach is good for smaller projects or those whose scope can be well-defined and less dynamic.

LOGICAL & LINEAR VS. SYSTEMS THINKING

Independent-minded brains are wired for logical and linear thinking. They break things down into components and then figure out each piece. They use stepwise thinking, going from a to b, b to c, c to d, etc. The logical and linear method is good for straightforward projects. This method can also be faster, taking less time to accomplish a goal.

Community thinkers, on the other hand, tend toward systems thinking, focusing on the entire outcome, including whether the performance specifications were met, but also whether relationships were preserved and individual accomplishments, like learning a new skill, were also met. This different focus achieves different results, and this approach can take more time and may be more resource intensive. The dichotomy for logical and linear vs. system thinking is shown in Figure 12.

Neither way is right or wrong. In fact, many studies have proven that having diverse thinking on the team produces the best results. Where you can leverage the tension between the two styles, you get superior results, because the tradeoffs get discussed and the knowledge from all parties gets incorporated into the final design.

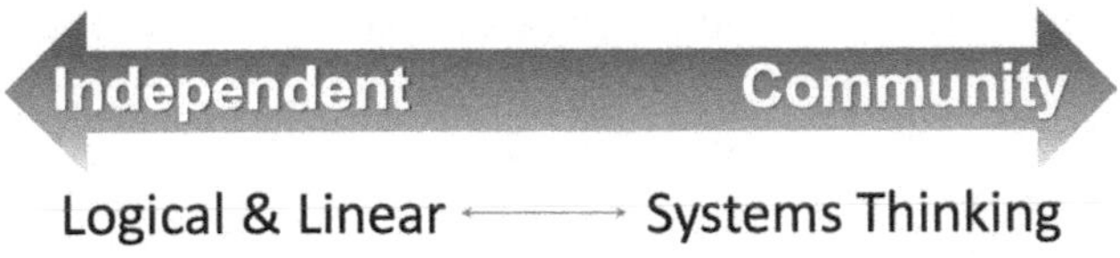

Logical & Linear ⟵⟶ Systems Thinking

Figure 12: Logical & Linear vs. Systems Thinking

***

Interestingly, most male brains tend to have seven times more gray matter, which is associated with concentrated attention on a specific action or task.[45] The female brain, on the other hand, can have ten times more white matter, which is what coordinates between the gray matter centers and may hypothetically give women a greater ability to switch between tasks and to multitask as well as deploy a systems thinking approach. Lifetime tracking suggests that balances of white and gray matter do shift over time.

***

What we need in the workplace is the right balance of these skills. We also need people who can work together to maximize their unique skills. The story below shows you how to leverage skills and apply systems thinking to deliver

45 Browning, Frank. The Fate of Gender; Nature, Nurture, and the Human Future. Bloomsbury USA, 2016.

incredible results. I found this example in the eye-opening book Presence: Human Purpose and the Field of the Future by Peter Senge.[46]

An MIT doctoral student named Daniel Kim set out to improve both the cost and time required to develop a new car. His team studied the development teams and tried to figure out what was keeping them from working together. They saw some disturbing patterns. Apparently, many teams were performing quick fixes that worked but weren't integrated within the whole system. To get a more fundamental solution required collaboration among the teams. The quick fixes resulted in unintended consequences, which were repaired with more quick fixes. The cycle perpetuated itself and rework just amped up the time pressure. This pattern had been created by the whole development team. At some point in the project, some of the team members realized:

"We are doing this to ourselves."

When they realized this reality, the "them"s became "us"s in their minds, and that was key to changing how people worked together. They finished the car development, one year earlier than the budgeted five years, and returned $63 million in allocated but unspent overrun costs.

---

46 Peter Senge, C. Otto Scharmer, Joseph Jaworski, and Betty Sue Flowers. Presence; Human Purpose and the Field of the Future. Society for Organizational Learning, 2004.

"When people who are actually creating a system start to see themselves as the source of their problems, they invariably discover a new capacity to create results they truly desire," Senge points out in his book.

PROCESSING SUMMARY

This chapter has covered a lot about how we think, process information, and prefer to work. I have taken each of the dichotomies that have been discussed and summarized them in Table 2. Keep in mind that the extremes are just that, and that we may find ourselves anywhere on any of these scales. Also, being in a certain place on one of these scales does not imply you are in the same place on another. Where you show up on the scale, may also be very situationally different. How you show up in the office and the PTA meeting may look very different.

The important thing is to start to understand your current style and know you can choose to function anywhere along the scale. To leverage gender differences, you need to also look at where you think other people fall on the scale. You can use your growing knowledge of how others process information in order to start a productive conversation about how you can work better together.

If we take all these characteristics together, we can create a framework that will help guide our understanding of our differences, as shown in Table 2.

How We Process

Process   Perceive   Value

Independent ←→ **Community**

Independent	Community
Independent ———→	Collaborative
Convergent ←———	Divergent
Bartering ————→	Sharing
Control ————→	Empowerment
Take Credit ———→	Give Credit
Divide & Conquer ——→	Share & Build
Logical & Linear ←—→	Systems Thinking

Table 2: Independent – vs. Community-Minded – Differences in How We Process Information and Work

CHAPTER 6

OUR DIFFERENCES: PERCEPTION

———

Imagination is more important than knowledge. For knowledge is limited, whereas imagination embraces the entire world, stimulating progress, giving birth to evolution.

—ALBERT EINSTEIN

Perception is the second category in our framework to understand our differences. This concept has a rather broad meaning, and I want to make sure it remains broad in your mind. Perception includes what you receive through your senses, the way you interpret what you have sensed (how it may alter your understanding), and how you react to that perception. It not only includes our five senses—sight, hearing, smell, taste, and touch—but also intuition, under-standing, and insight.

Perception is like a lens we peer through that frames what we see in a certain way. When two people see the same object or situation in radically different ways, their communication becomes garbled. Have you ever seen two people who are in "violent agreement"? I've seen countless examples in meetings. Two people usually start arguing about some specific point they disagree on. As the discussion carries on, they continue to argue, moving on to different points. Eventually, they are arguing with each other so vehemently over the details that they don't even realize they are arguing the same side. I find it quite amusing to "break it up" by letting them know they actually concur with each other on the overall direction to be taken but disagree on a few points. They are usually so engrossed in the details and the argument that I find I have to repeat myself two or three times before they actually hear what I am saying.

In her book That's What She Said, Joanne Lipman writes,[47]

"One out of five men in a global survey of more than 17,000 people in 24 countries said women are inferior to men. Almost half of women as well as men

---

47 Lipman, Joanne. That's What She Said: What Men Need to Know (And Women Need to Tell Them) About Working Together. Harper Collins Publishers, 2018.

surveyed in Russia and India believe women to be inferior. And this was a survey done in 2017."

Catalyst's survey found that an astonishing 51 percent of men cited lack of awareness about exactly which issues women are facing.[48]

A Yale study found that male executives who spoke more than their peers were viewed as more competent. For female executives, the reverse was true: if they spoke more than their peers, they were judged as 14 percent less competent. A 2012 study found that men speak a whopping 75 percent of the time, and that women as a result have little impact on decisions.[49]

Do these facts shock you? They stunned me when I first read them. None of us want to believe that's true in the professional working world we've created, but the truth is right here in front of us. Our biases are showing! Is this the legacy we want to leave our children? It doesn't have to be this way; we can change it.

Matt Krentz leads the People Team for the Boston Consulting Group (BCG). When he took a hard look at their own behavior he realized, "we need to change the environment in which we work, how we give feedback, and more proactively engage on how we are mentoring, sponsoring, guiding

---

48 Ibid.
49 Ibid.

women." The bottom line is "our male leaders need to be engaged on this," Matt said. "We have to behave differently." Matt decided to focus on driving improvements at the company. From 2011 to 2016, the number of female consultants grew by 70 percent—quite an impressive leap.[50]

We can see positive progress occurring; it's just not wide or deep enough to make a difference yet. So how do we get there?

Lipman really nails this issue in her book:[51]

"Men have grown up that equal at work means the same — that does a disservice to us all. It doesn't allow for the many differences that may inadvertently reward men while penalizing women. It smooths over and negates the challenges that women face every day, which in turn makes their experience invisible to men."

"Invisible to men"—that's certainly a part of the problem, but we need to contend with some other facets as well. Therese Huston succinctly summarized a big part of the problem in her book like this:[52]

---

50 Ibid.
51 Ibid.
52 Huston, Therese. How Women Decide; What's True, What's Not, and What Strategies Spark the Best Choices. Mariner Books, 2016.

"Society has been underestimating women's abilities to make astute choices for years, and this doubting, this routine questioning of a women's judgment, drives many of the gender differences we see."

I get that it is difficult sometimes to understand another person's perspective. After all, can you really "live in another's shoes"? Today, many transgender people are willing to share their stories. I use their stories to shed some light on what we can't see for ourselves. Their narratives add clarity and illuminate our limited perspectives, because they are people who have not only walked in other's shoes, but also lived on both sides of the gender divide.

I met Jay Pryor (whose pronouns are they/them) at the Wonder Women in Tech Conference. I was attending as a panelist and blown away by Jay's speech. The first aspect was their ability to be so incredibly vulnerable both on stage and in person. Jay is good-looking, with red hair and a nicely trimmed beard. Their twenty-minute speech, titled "Woman in Man Skin: A Narrative on Gender Consciousness," was revealing in ways that were so authentic, I found it transformative. Let's start with a bit of background on Jay:

According to their speaker bio,

"Born female, Jay transitioned to male after 35 years of living life as a woman. Living as a gender non-conforming person grants them truly unique insight into how differently women experience the world versus men, the challenges that the LGBT+ community face daily and how those challenges translate to the work force."

I spoke with Jay after the conference. They were a project director for a company that designs the interiors for offices—you know the infamous cubes we have all come to recognize and wish were something else. Before the transition, when presenting as a woman, Jay would make remarks in meetings and have male clients frequently respond like: "I'll need to check with the general contractor [or the electrician, or the foreman] on that." Such reactions happened often, and of course, Jay assumed everyone experienced them. Luckily for the purposes of our understanding, Jay kept the same role during and after their transition. While they were essentially the same person, doing the same job, now they had a completely different appearance, a "Woman in Man Skin." Now when Jay went to a meeting and made the same statements, a funny thing happened: no one second-guessed or even questioned what Jay had said. What "he" said was now taken as a fact. He perceived "he" was the expert, but "she" was not.

Even in my own life, I have experienced this phenomenon. My boss and I were at a client meeting. I had just finished giving a four-hour technical presentation through which my boss had sat very quietly. One of the clients in the room began their questions by asking my boss a question. He said, "I believe Karen just shared four hours of the technical details with you; she is the expert." I then answered the question. The next question from another gentleman was directed at my boss. This time he simply said, "I defer to Karen" and made a gesture with his hand, palm up, fingers pointing at me. The third time this happened, he didn't even say anything, just made the same hand gesture. Finally, the fourth question was actually directed to me, for the first time. My boss was quite an amazing person and an enlightened manager. The stance he took was perfect and his redirection of the questions straightforward and validating. But, why did the other men in the room continue to ask him the questions, three times in a row?

Have you ever seen this happen?

All these behaviors revolve around perception differences. This chapter is designed to help you see some prevalent perception differences. As you hear about some of these, you'll begin to see them for yourself at your workplace and at social events. I encourage you to be curious about these and to ask questions. Whenever we can open up dialogue on these topics, we become better informed. We begin to understand our perception differences. In our dialogue, we will find the deeper meaning behind the behavior we see and have been reacting to, and that may just alter our perception enough to look at things differently.

Let's take an example that has been touted in the press to demonstrate the perception difference. This case is another great excerpt drawn from Huston's book How Women Decide:[53]

"Best Buy CEO Hubert Joly decided a week after Marissa Mayer's 'no work from home policy' to enact the same policy. His act was discussed briefly for a few months. Hers is still being talked about. So, for making the same judgment call, a male CEO drew sidelong glances for a few months, but a female CEO drew extensive scrutiny and censure for years.

"Both had been in their jobs about 6 months. One likely reason we keep fuming over Mayer's decision but ignore Joly's choice lies in a pattern that many of us unknowingly fall into: we're quick to question a women's decision but inclined to accept a man's. Men and women don't have to act differently for us to see them differently."

This chapter is designed to make you aware of some of these common patterns around perceptions.

As you begin to open dialogue about these issues, you need to be aware that not everyone will agree with you. You should know that even high-profile men who have reached across the gender divide have been attacked on social media. It's all about perception, right?

Robert Moritz, CEO of Price Waterhouse Coopers (PwC) wrote a LinkedIn post about why the firm values diversity. Commenters on the post, who were other professional men,

---

53   Ibid.

using their own real names, called his ideas "repellent" and "an affront to every white man"; in addition to arguing "there's no such thing as a real business run by a non-white man," one even suggested he "surrender [his] job to a diversity hire and stay at home as a house husband."[54]

What are the biggest obstacles holding us back? Why haven't we been able to make improvements in this area? As Lipman describes in her book:

> "Catalyst asked men what might undermine their support for equality, a stunning 74% cited fear — fear of loss of status, fear of other men's disapproval, and most telling of all, fear of making a mistake. Men are walking around on eggshells."

Men may be walking around on eggshells, but women are being denied the opportunity to fully participate. We deserve that right, and our kids should not have to fight this battle in the workplaces they enter. We owe it to them to fix this issue while we are in the workforce. This disparity is not something our kids should inherit from us.

***

---

54 Lipman, Joanne. That's What She Said: What Men Need to Know (And Women Need to Tell Them) About Working Together. Harper Collins Publishers, 2018.

One of the things I often find is that a little bit of information can go a long way in helping us to understand where people are coming from. Our perceptions can dramatically change if we take the time to try and understand others' viewpoints.

My dad spent his last years in an assisted-living facility near my home. I visited nearly every day and got to know quite a few of the residents. One spry gentleman living there intrigued me. He could be quippy with his remarks. Often, if I got in the elevator and he was there, I'd ask, "How are you today, Max?" His response was always the same: "I'm alive." This first few times he gave this response, I thought that was an odd greeting, and rather abrupt. I had trouble continuing the conversation, not really knowing what to say next.

Then, one day I got in the elevator and saw an announcement about a book talk for Auschwitz, Auschwitz: I Cannot Forget You...As Long As I Remain Alive, so I signed up to attend. The author was Max.[55] He was an Auschwitz survivor, tattoo and all. His talk was both inspiring and frightening; it was my first detailed venture into a part of our history that I may never be able to comprehend. I bought his book and read it, mesmerized by his story, the atrocities, and his amazing perseverance.

The next time I saw Max in the hallway, I asked, "How are you today, Max?" His usual response, "I'm alive," took on

55 Garcia, Priscilla Alden Thwaits. Auschwitz, Auschwitz...I Cannot Forget You: As Long As I Remain Alive". Social Thinking Press, 2008.

a completely different meaning for me. A little information can completely change your perception.

***

This chapter is broken down into three parts. Each section discusses different ways our perceptions color our world. In the first section, I discuss what I call mindset perceptions. Our mindsets represent an established set of attitudes that we hold. The work of Carol Dweck brought mindset into our lexicon with her fixed and growth mindset dichotomy. However, I am going back to tap into the work of a well know linguist, Deborah Tannen, who studied differences between how men and women use language...very differently.

The second section picks up several areas where men and women diverge, sometimes dramatically, in their perceptions of a given situation. This section includes some bizarre anomalies around our abilities to estimate, how we get tripped up by blind spots, and few other perception differences that are often tied to gender.

The third section is an interesting compilation of items where people seem to be applying rather different yardsticks (or criteria for what success looks like) depending on whether the behavior is exhibited by a man or woman. The existence of these different yardsticks begs the question: how should we judge success? And should men and women be judged differently?

MINDSET PERCEPTIONS

In this section, we'll cover several dichotomies around perception where we frequently find ourselves on opposite extremes. Keep in mind that I'll be describing some of the extremes, but most people will find themselves somewhere between the two. Again, nothing is right or wrong about either side. The point is that a whole spectrum of mindset perceptions exists. The more we are aware of others' perceptions, the more likely we are to extend our empathy to them, relate to them, and be able to see them as a fellow human being who sees the world differently.

Deborah Tannen, professor of linguistics at Georgetown University, has done in-depth studies of the differences in communication between men and women, likening them to cross-cultural communication issues seen between cultures.[56]

Tannen's work highlights the different focus that the two genders take in conversation. Because both groups have a different underlying purpose for conversation, it becomes easy to misinterpret meaning when looking through one's own lens. These misinterpretations have caused and continue to cause multitudes of disagreements between men and women.

According to Tannen, men's conversations are used to establish their status, or where they sit in the pecking order of men: who is up and who is down. Women, on the other

---

56 Tannen, Deborah. You Just Don't Understand: Women and Men in Conversation. Ballantine Books, 1990.

hand, use conversations to establish a connection to others. Just the juxtaposition between these two underlying motives for a conversation can make your head spin, even before anyone utters a word.

STATUS VS. CONNECTION AND INDEPENDENCE VS. INTERDEPENDENCE

Tannen uses an interesting example in her book. It's telling how the same information can appear very different to different people. Tannen read a journal article by a woman who thanked her husband in the acknowledgement section for his helpful discussions with her on the book topic. Tannen thought it was a nice way for the author to acknowledge and thank her husband. When one of her male colleagues first read this acknowledgement, however, he thought the author must be incompetent or at least insecure, because of the same acknowledgement!

Imagine how often the community-minded, who think they are displaying a positive quality like connection, are misjudged by the independent-minded, who perceive them as revealing a lack of necessary independence, which the independent-minded regard as synonymous with incompetence and insecurity.

Likewise, the independent-minded may display their knowledge by "offering" solutions to the community-minded when they talk about their problems. Unfortunately, you'll see that the community-minded may really have been expecting

understanding rather than solutions. These mindset perceptions can really throw us off!

One of the characteristics of the independent-minded
is they want to maintain their independence and freedom,
sometimes at all costs, while our community-minded revere
interdependence; their intimacy with others is what makes
them thrive.

Tannen clarifies the difference well:

> "The point is not that women do not value free-
> dom or that men do not value connection to others.
> It is rather that the desire for freedom and indepen-
> dence becomes more of an issue for many men in
> relationships, whereas interdependence and connec-
> tion become more of an issue for many women. The
> difference is on focus and degree."

When either person encounters the other's style, they
judge them by their own standards of conversational style.
The community-minded show concern by following up
on "trouble talk" and asking additional questions about
the troubles expressed. In this way, they show that they
care and are listening. The points they make will be to
sympathize with the other person, like: "That must have
made you feel awful," which validates the other person and
offers intimacy, suggesting, "I understand what you are
going through."

When this same conversation happens between a community-minded and an independent-minded thinker, you often get a radically different but equally perplexing outcome. Frequently, you will find that when the community-minded starts asking questions of the independent-minded, the independent-minded will change the subject, avoiding a potential discussion about emotions that is of much less importance to them. When the independent-minded person changes the subject abruptly, the community-minded one believes they are showing a lack of sympathy and experience a failure of intimacy.

If we flip the situation around and have a community-minded thinker who opens up to discuss issues, we often find that the independent-minded person wants to jump in and "solve" the problem; they want to "fix it." However, the community thinker is not necessarily looking for a solution—more often than not, they are really looking for some sympathy, understanding, reassurance, or intimacy. When they get a solution instead, they get frustrated and think the independent-minded person just doesn't care. Once this response occurs, the independent-minded who just offered up a perfectly valid solution, which seems to have been rejected outright, is now totally baffled. They are thinking: "You told me about your problem, I offered you a perfectly good solution, and your response is 'You just don't care about me'? What?"

This type of conversation can take another type of turn too. Let's say a community-minded person talks about their problem to an independent-minded person. The independent-minded thinker then says, "Oh, it's not that bad; I've seen worse." (This would be a typical response between two independent-minded people who often play the "I can top that one" status game.) But the community-minded now feels belittled, like their feelings have been discounted. This example also shows how the independent-minded was actually trying to make the conversation symmetrical but ended up inadvertently creating a very asymmetrical one.

Figure 13 shows the two dichotomies of status vs. connection and independence vs. interdependence.

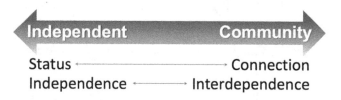

Figure 13: Status vs. Connection and Independence vs. Interdependence

One of the biggest overarching themes in Tannen's work is the focus that the independent-minded put on their status and the focus that the community-minded put on connections or relationships. The independent-minded need others to see them as equal or better, so they are not inclined to do anything that may lower their status in the eyes of others. Their credibility and self-image are always on the line. The other characteristic that the independent-minded prize is their independence—it is interwoven into their status. They want to make their own decisions, they don't want help, and they certainly don't want to be told what to do. They feel that their independence being threatened could lower their status and push them down.

The community-minded, on the other hand, always want to build and preserve their relationships. They do everything they can to level the playing field and put people on an equal footing. What's most important is that the lines of communication are open. While the independent-minded want independence, the community-minded need interdependence to ensure the needs of the community are being met.

TELLING VS. ASKING

Now we get to have some fun with one of life's burning questions: why do the independent-minded resist asking for directions? And, for that matter, why does it not bother the community-minded at all to ask? These questions constitute one of the paradoxes of independence and intimacy. Apparently, very different meta-messages are implied when you ask for or give information to another person. According to Tannen:

"When you offer information, the information itself is the message. But the fact that you have the information, and the person you are speaking to doesn't, also sends a meta-message of superiority," she explains. "If relations are inherently hierarchical, then the one who has more information is framed as higher up on the ladder by virtue of being more knowledgeable and competent. From this perspective, finding one's own way is an essential part of the independence that men perceive to be a prerequisite for self-respect. If self-respect is bought at the cost of a few extra minutes of travel time, it is well worth the price."

Figure 14 depicts the telling vs. asking dichotomy.

Figure 14: Telling vs. Asking

This conversation has an interesting flip side, related to how the community-minded share information they know with the independent-minded. First off, they are cautious about this sharing—remember, they want to maintain an equal status for all. Let's picture a community-minded person as a passenger who has been to their destination many times before. The independent-minded thinker is the driver in this case, who has never been and does not know how to get there. The independent-minded would need to ask the community-minded if they had advice on the best route to take. The community-minded would offer directions but would probably add something like: "That's how I would go, but there might be a better way." This comment accomplishes two things: it can help to restore an equal status to the conversation, but it also allows the community-minded to save face, while at the same time giving permission to the independent-minded to choose another route.

As we move through some of these examples, you may find yourself "replaying" some of your recent conversations and suddenly able to see them in a completely new light.

ASYMMETRY VS. SYMMETRY

The independent-minded need to establish asymmetry in their relationships. It's all part of knowing the hierarchy. Conversely, for the community-minded, it's all about maintaining symmetry in relationships. The community-minded are not inclined to flaunt their knowledge, because it creates asymmetries they would then need to fix, which is why, until we get our work cultures adjusted, you may need to continue to ask some people to speak up in meetings and conversations to get all the knowledge on the table.

Tannen summarized this with the following analogy, suggesting that "the game women play is 'Do you like me?' Whereas the men play 'Do you respect me?' If men, in seeking respect, are less liked by women, this is an unsought side effect, as is the effect that women, in seeking to be liked, may lose respect. When a woman has a conversation with a man, her efforts to emphasize their similarities and avoid showing off can easily be interpreted through the lens of status, as relegating her to a one-down position, making her appear either incompetent or insecure." Figure 15 shows the asymmetry vs. symmetry dichotomy.

Figure 15: Asymmetry vs. Symmetry

These conversational traits are all interrelated. Interdependence is symmetrical. To maintain this condition, people are dependent on each other: both people need each other, and neither is one-up nor one-down. Status and independence are asymmetrical. One person needs the other, but not vice versa. The differing goals of symmetry and asymmetry are usually unstated and undetected during conversation, hence neither party acknowledges nor understands the reasons for the other person's behavior. What's even worse is that these differing goals result in alignments that enhance the authority of the independent-minded and undercut the authority of the community-minded.

REPORT TALK VS. RAPPORT TALK

The independent-minded prefer to do what Tannen calls "report talk." Specifically, they like to speak in public, and the more people they speak to, the better. This interest includes both public speaking and speaking in groups where you do not know people well. When the independent-minded talk, they do so to preserve their independence and to either negotiate or maintain their hierarchy in the group, so they must exhibit their knowledge and skill, which is why Tannen calls this report talk. It is much more like "reporting out" information. The content of report talk tends to be technical and impersonal. The independent-minded have learned to use talking as a way to get and keep other people's attention.

The community-minded talk in a different way, "rapport talk." The intent of rapport talk is to establish rapport and connection. By nature, rapport talk is more effective with smaller groups of people and hence more like private than public speaking. Rapport talk tends to include content of a more personal nature. It's not just what happened in the meeting; it includes how you felt about what was discussed and what the possible ramifications might be. The community-minded are more comfortable talking when they are among friends and equals and when they feel safe to share.

Figure 16 shows the report talk vs. rapport talk dichotomy.

Report Talk ←——————→ Rapport Talk

Figure 16: Report vs. Rapport Talk

Among the status-seeking report talkers is an interest-ing dynamic we can observe. When an independent-minded person begins to lecture, holding the floor, the other indepen-dent-minded people will attempt to sidetrack them, match them in the conversation, and even derail the conversation. A bit of "let me top that story" goes on, which is the way they exchange information. Also, listening is passive and considered submissive, so these engagements are also a way to establish their status.

For the community-minded, the protocol is to wait for your turn to talk. Well, if the independent-minded never cede the floor, the community-minded will find it difficult to make their point and often find themselves listening to what seems like a lecture. Additionally, most community-minded people lack experience in defending themselves against challenges, intentional sidetracking, or conversation-derailing attempts. In fact, they often misinterpret these as personal attacks on their credibility.

When a mixture of independent – and communi-ty-minded people are together, they are judged by the rules of the independent-minded, which are considered the norm

in business, leaving the community-minded in a bit of a dou-
ble bind. If they speak like the community-minded, they are
seen as inadequate leaders; if they speak like the independent-minded they are seen as stepping out of their role, trying
to be someone they are not.

> *"The road to authority is tough for women*
> *and once they get there it's a bed of thorns."*
>
> – DEBORAH TANNEN

DIRECT VS. INDIRECT

The independent-minded tend to state directly what they
want, like "I'm hungry; let's stop and get some food," while
the community-minded communicate in a more indirect
manner. They might say, "Oh, look, there are some restau-
rants at the next exit." The independent-minded may not
know what this statement means. After all, the other person
is simply pointing out a fact, so they may keep driving, at
which point the community-minded, believing they made
a request that was ignored, may become upset because the
other person did not seem to want to respond and perhaps
did not care about the needs they thought they just expressed.

The independent-minded have an early warning system
that detects other people telling them what to do. Being told
what to do is an affront to their independence. What's more,

if it is being done indirectly, the action is even worse, as they may believe the other person is trying to manipulate them and control their behavior.

The community-minded have an early warning system that detects asymmetries and makes attempts to maintain the symmetry in relationships. Realizing that telling people what to do is asymmetrical and hierarchical, they attempt to level the playing field by making their requests indirectly.

The irony is that these two approaches, while both attempting to "maintain their styles," are actually making the situation worse.

Figure 17 shows the direct vs. indirect dichotomy.

Figure 17: Direct vs. Indirect

FACTS VS. FEELINGS

The independent-minded like to discuss information and facts, which might include what is happening in business, politics, and sports. They do not like to discuss their personal relationships, and if these are brought up, they will be discussed only briefly without elaboration or details. Their conversations tend be informational with impersonal, factual, and task-focused content.

The community-minded's conversations center around personal content. For example, if you are talking about your vacation, they want to hear about your experience in that foreign country. They are not interested as much in a list of the cities that you visited or a bunch of factual information, but more in what you found interesting in those cities. What did you enjoy, what surprised you, what would you do again and why? The facts vs. feelings dichotomy is shown in Figure 18.

Figure 18: Facts vs. Feelings

You can see that when you try to put these styles together you end up with some inherent conflicts, because the two types of thinkers have very different ideas of "what" is important to communicate.

SUMMARY OF MINDSET PERCEPTIONS

Deborah Tannen has done some amazing work to pick apart what happens in everyday conversation between people. She has been able to capture many nuances in conversations that many of us fail to see even when they are staring us in the face. More than just linguistic nuances, much of her work is an indicator of mindset. Any time you can understand how people perceive the world, you are in a much better position to realize what drives them and influence their thinking.

I constructed the table below from Deborah's book You Just Don't Understand.[57] I extracted several characteristics discussed above that she described in her book and then incorporated them into our dichotomy scales to highlight these differences.

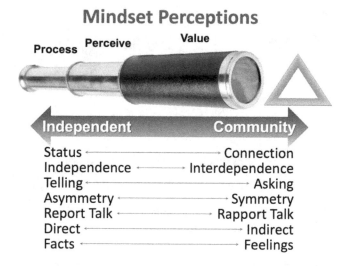

Table 3: Mindset Perceptions Based on Conversational Purpose

57 Ibid.

Let's move beyond language and conversation and take a look at some other perception differences prevalent in our society.

PERCEPTION DIFFERENCES

Several differences we experience seem to indicate that men and women have drastic differences in how they perceive the same situation. As I did my research, I uncovered a whole set of these differing perceptions, and I describe them here. This section includes five specific areas I have identified thus far: estimating, blind spots, externalize or internalize, intuition, and apologizing.

ESTIMATING

Some interesting work has emerged from the film industry, recently.

The Geena Davis Institute on Gender in Media found that, on average, only 17 percent of the people in the film crew's scenes are female, but the perception of men is that there are 50 percent women.[58]

---

58 Lipman, Joanne. That's What She Said: What Men Need to Know (And Women Need to Tell Them) About Working Together. Harper Collins Publishers, 2018.

Apparently, when we look at the same situations, we often walk away with major perception differences. Try to wrap your head around these:

From a survey of 3,000 employees of business or law firms, we get the following statistic: 54 percent of the men surveyed said men and women are allies in reaching gender equality, yet only 31 percent of women agreed.[59]

Another study cited in Lipman's book revealed other statistics that make one stop to think, What is really going on here?

"One study found that men routinely overestimate their IQ by five points, while women underestimate theirs by the same amount," Lipman explains. "In another experiment, after men and women each took a math test, men overestimated their performance by 30%, twice as much as women did. Let's be clear, the men aren't lying. They believe that they performed better than they did."[60]

---

59 Rubino, Kathryn, "ABA Survey Reveals Men think they're doing a pretty good job being allies to Women. Women Disagree." Above the Law, Aug 7, 2018.

60 Lipman, Joanne. That's What She Said: What Men Need to Know (And Women Need to Tell Them) About Working Together. Harper Collins Publishers, 2018.

Can our perceptions really be that far off?

Tasha Eurich, in her book Insight about our self-awareness and the importance of its role in business and life, offers this:[61]

> *"The least competent people tend to be the most confident in their abilities."*

This phenomenon is so prevalent that it even has a name: the Dunning-Kruger Effect. How does this happen? Eurich contends that "the incompetent are not lying about their abilities, it is more likely that they are blessed with inappropriate confidence, buoyed by something that feels … like knowledge."

Another huge perception difference feeds this, according to Lipman: "Men overestimate the number of women and their career progress."

We believe this misconception happens because a man may see one woman in a high-level position, then assume that other women occupy similar positions. Men are "filling in the voids" of information in a way that matches their experience, not realizing their experience is much different than women's.[62]

---

61 Eurich, Tasha. Insight. Crown Business, 2017.
62 Lipman, Joanne. That's What She Said: What Men Need to Know (And Women Need to Tell Them) About Working Together. Harper Collins Publishers, 2018.

BLIND SPOTS

It ain't what you don't know that gets you into trouble. It's what you know for sure that just ain't so.

—JOSH BILLINGS

A lot of hidden assumptions are out there, and apparently men and women have their own sets of assumptions that diverge significantly. We use these expectations to establish our own distinct secret decoder or frame of reference, which we then use to interpret the world. Each of us carries around this view or frame and applies it to our everyday interactions. The problem is that all of our decoders are different, yet we repeatedly assume that others see our view. It's a wonder we can get along at all.

To make matter worse, take a look at these startling facts, from Eurich's book:[63]

In one study of more than 13,000 professionals in financial services and tech, nursing, and others, researchers found almost no relationship between self-assessed performance and objective performance ratings. They dubbed this the "Steve disease." A characteristic of people with the Steve disease is complete confidence in their self-views, all of which are completely wrong.

---

63 Eurich, Tasha. Insight. Crown Business, 2017.

Eurich believes we all suffer from three blind spots, which is why we're so terrible at evaluating our own performance. One of the problems with this is, according to Eurich:

"The more we ignore the Three Blindspots, the more pernicious they become."

The first is knowledge blindness. In specific situations, the opinions we have about our abilities are based more on the general beliefs we have about ourselves and our underlying skills and less on how we actually perform. The more expertise, the more blindness. More often than we think, the experts are wrong.

An investigation of nearly 1,000 engineers in the San Francisco Bay Area revealed that more than 33 percent rated their performance in the top 5 percent relative to their peers. Only one brave soul labeled himself as below average.

Emotional blindness is second. This type manifests itself as follows: when we ask ourselves how happy we are with our life, the answer we get is based more on the mood we are in at the time we are asked the question. We are not aware of how our emotions affect our judgment.

Finally, there's behavior blindness, which stems from the fact that it's hard to see yourself as the audience does. You can't objectively evaluate yourself. Thus, organizations like Toastmasters International rely on evaluations from the audience as feedback. They have recognized that our view of ourselves is not the same as the way the audience sees us. Perhaps more importantly, what comes out of our mouths is nowhere near as important as what lands in our listeners' ears, heads, and hearts.

The Steve disease is usually a combination of these blind spots. Learning the truth gives us the power to improve. The more aware we are of these blind spots, the better chance we have to overcome them.

Some pretty severe consequences in our companies are a direct result of the Steve disease. According to Eurich:[64]

> "Employees who lack self-awareness bring down team performance, reduce decision quality by an average of 36%, hurting coordination by 46%, and increasing conflict by 30%."

Financial performance for these companies is much worse. One study involving hundreds of publicly traded companies found that those with poor financial returns were 79 percent more likely to have large numbers of employees who lack self-awareness. As Eurich describes:

> *"The big Catch-22 of self-awareness is that the people who need it the most are usually the least likely to know they need it."*

---

64 Ibid.

One of the most significant differences between the self-aware and everybody else is the commitment to learn and accept reality. Of course, the first step is to identify the assumptions we are making about ourselves and the world around us.

EXTERNALIZE VS. INTERNALIZE

There are a few gender facts that most people agree on, and this concept is one of them. The independent-minded tend to externalize, and the community-minded tend to internalize. Let's picture an independent – and community minded person, both arriving late for an important meeting. From the independent-minded, you might hear, "I'm late because traffic was just awful." From the community-minded, "Sorry, I was late. I didn't leave home early enough. I knew I should have left earlier because traffic can be so unpredictable, and I knew this meeting was important."

The focus for independent-minded is on themselves, whereas for the community-minded the focus is on others. We use our focuses to explain when something goes wrong. The community-minded tend to blame themselves; the independent-minded blame others or extenuating circumstances.

Interestingly, when things go right—by which I mean great—a whole different behavior enters the picture. Let's say a community-minded and an independent-minded person each deliver an outstanding presentation. In this case, oddly enough, a community-minded person is likely to pull the "luck" card. "It all just came together. My team was great, and I was lucky." For the independent-minded, this success is a great status symbol, so of course, it was all the result of their hard work. This phenomenon harkens back to Deborah Tannen's model, in which the independent-minded seek status and the community-minded seek connection. Both of these reactions to positive outcomes allow each person to maintain their desired positions (high status for the independent-minded, and establishing connection and preserving their relationships for the community-minded).

INTUITION

Women's intuition has often been brought up in discussions on gender differences. The book How We Decide, includes some interesting insight.[65]

A columnist from Psychology Today says, "Women practice this mantra: trust your inner knowledge, your intuition, that gut feeling," and in the same article it says we should let others know when we are making a decision based on our intuition. But, as we know, feelings and emotions are not currently credible in the business world. But they should be.

So, what is intuition? While many feel it is some kind of magical power, it is not. Our brains process information without our awareness all the time. Have you ever left work

---

65 Huston, Therese. How Women Decide; What's True, What's Not, and What Strategies Spark the Best Choices. Mariner Books, 2016.

and arrived home without any recollection of the drive? Your driving went on autopilot, and your brain proceeded to launch into unconscious processing mode. You are usually not even aware it's happening.

Intuition happens as your brain looks at past experience and knowledge you've accumulated, along with your current emotions and cues from your environment. It is not a decision that you make by consciously reasoning through the data; it happens in your "gut." That person makes me nervous, or I really like this person even though we just met. Often, if a decision was made intuitively, the person may not be able to articulate the reason they made it, because of course it happened unconsciously—we don't actually know why we decided that way.

Are women more intuitive than men? After all, for years, it has been called "women's intuition." Women may be more intuitive simply because they allow themselves to feel their emotions and may be more in touch with themselves. A big piece of intuition comes from being in touch with your surroundings and reading other people's emotions. Women's corpus callosums, which connect the left logical side of the brain to the right sensing and emotional side of the brain, are larger, and that connectivity may also contribute to higher levels of intuition.

Men express their feelings all the time, but they do so less directly and less openly than women do. Men are more likely to joke, drink, or just fall silent when they are feeling depressed. Under the same conditions, women prefer to talk about their anxieties and fears. This talk may also give them an advantage in differentiating emotions, simply because they have had more practice doing it.

Being able to read others' emotions is a useful skill, particularly in the workplace; it can allow you to not just keep your job but also to climb the career ladder. Sara Snodgrass studied Harvard students, pairing them up and telling one of the pair they were in charge, the boss. She expected that the women would have the upper hand in reading nonverbal cues from the designated leader but ended up with a surprising outcome. It turns out that the subordinates, whether they were men or women, had the better ability to read the nonverbal cues and emotions, demonstrating that men can learn how to read emotions and nonverbal cues. In her study, Sara thought we should call it "subordinates' intuition" instead of women's intuition. After all, when the man was working for the woman, he was able to read her cues.

An interesting side note on intuition: Albert Einstein was an amazing person and unique in many ways. Based on all his scientific discoveries, one might think that he was totally left-brained. Here, however, is one of his quotes:

"The intuitive mind is a sacred gift and the rational mind is a faithful servant. We have created a society that honors the servant and has forgotten the gift."

It turns out that Einstein was quite intuitive and used those powers to come up with theories that totally bucked traditional thinking, such as his theory of relativity.

APOLOGIZING

The community-minded are known to apologize, a lot, especially compared to the independent-minded. Apologies are used by the community-minded to level imbalances in relationships that may occur. Also, realize that the words "I'm sorry" have two meanings: one is an apology, and the other is to express sympathy or concern. That's why people say, "I am so sorry," when someone passes away; in that instance, the phrase does not indicate they feel responsible for the death, but instead that they empathize with the person and recognize they are experiencing a lot of strong feelings.

The independent-minded do not apologize unless they have made a mistake and they wish to admit fault. This concession will, in their minds, also lower their status, which may be why we hear apologies much less frequently from them.[66]

Realize that when an independent-minded person hears the community-minded person's apology, they may think, "Why would you lower your status for that?" (noting that they themselves would not apologize for something like that).

66 Tannen, Deborah. You Just Don't Understand: Women and Men in Conversation. Ballantine Books, 1990.

"You must not think very highly of yourself, so I won't either" is the implication. It puts a different twist on things, don't you think?

A DIFFERENT YARDSTICK

As I collected all kinds of gender differences to discuss in this book, I realized I had amassed a whole set of differences that had an uncommon distinction: that people seem to be using completely different yardsticks to measure performance depending on your gender, almost as if two completely different sets of criteria exist. Even more confounding is that certain behaviors get judged one way if you are woman and a completely different way if you are a man. I guess as long as you are calling us inconsistent, then you will be right.

INTERRUPTIONS

Kieran Snyder, a tech executive with a Ph.D. in linguistics, did a study in her own company. She calculated interruptions in meetings and found that men were three times more likely to interrupt women than other men. The few women who do interrupt overwhelmingly interrupted other women, a stunning 87 percent of the time. They almost never interrupted men.[67]

---

67 Lipman, Joanne. That's What She Said: What Men Need to Know (And Women Need to Tell Them) About Working Together. Harper Collins Publishers, 2018.

Northwestern University did an analysis of Supreme Court arguments. The researchers reviewed over a dozen years of data and found the three female justices were interrupted three times more frequently than their male counterparts.[68]

Katherine Hilton did a fascinating study while at Stanford, surveying 5,000 people to determine what affects how people perceive interruptions.[69]

"Gendered ways of talking and interpreting matter, and they have many consequences, including political ones," assistant linguistics professor Rob Podesva said. "Katherine's research shows that there are systematic gender disparities in how we interpret interruptions. Being aware of these disparities may be the first step in figuring out how to address them in the future."

"Male listeners were more likely to view a female speaker who interrupted as ruder, less friendly and less intelligent than if the interrupter were male, although both male and female speakers were performing identical scripts in the audio clips," according to Hilton. Furthermore, "female listeners did not show a significant bias in favor of female or male speakers."

---

68 Ibid.
69 Shashkevich, Alex, "Researcher examines how people perceive interruptions in conversation." Stanford University, May 2, 2018.

"Finding this gender bias wasn't as surprising as the extent of it and the fact that it altered perceptions of a female speaker's intelligence, which we don't think of as related to interruptions," Hilton explained.

DON'T CROSS THAT LINE! – THE RESPECT GAP

An incredibly baffling phenomenon contrasts what happens between community – and independent-minded people. Apparently, when a woman displays tendencies typically characterized as male or a man displays characteristics typically associated with women, people of the opposite sex object. When either blatantly demonstrates the proclivities of the other, immediate retribution follows from people who think the opposite.

As Lipman wrote in her book: "79% of male supervisors reported worrying about giving women candid feedback and said they felt they had to provide guidance carefully and indirectly. The irony is that by self-censoring, the men don't give women feedback necessary for the women to advance."[70]

If you go back to Deborah Tannen's linguistic model, you find that independent-minded are direct, while the community-minded are more indirect. The example above

---

70 Lipman, Joanne. That's What She Said: What Men Need to Know (And Women Need to Tell Them) About Working Together. Harper Collins Publishers, 2018.

represents the independent-minded attempting to speak like a community-minded person in order to be heard when offering feedback. The subtle undertone is that doing so is difficult, so how many independent-minded people will attempt it to get their message across? Most seem to feel it is easier to just take the silent route, which also, unfortunately, deprives the community-minded of the feedback they need to improve.

In the working world, many of us have grown up understanding that we need to tell people exactly what they need to get better at doing. Many community-minded people can be devastated when they hear this news the first time. This direct feedback method is great for the independent-minded as it is their preferred communication mode, but it can be alienating to the community minded.[71]

Researchers discovered that some community-minded people react to negative feedback far more strongly than the independent-minded. Interestingly, when given a mix of positive and negative feedback, the community-minded put greater weight on the negative while the independent-minded focus on the positive feedback.[72]

Community-minded people who are direct, like the independent-minded, are labeled as uncaring and insensitive. The community-minded in positions of power who assert their

---

71 Ibid.
72 Ibid.

authority are inevitably punished for it. Many studies have been performed verifying that the community-minded are penalized for behaviors considered stereotypically "independent," including being direct, assertive, and self-promotional. One meta-analysis looked at seventy-one studies of assertive behavior and found that women, not men, are looked down upon for basic behaviors like: negotiating for a raise or even something as mundane as asking someone to turn down their music.[73]

What is fascinating are some of the contrasts between the interpretation of the gender differences.

When men get angry at work, they are given greater respect by others—a reality verified by three separate studies. But when women get angry on the job, watch out: they get less respect. Men's anger is attributed to external causes (i.e., they had a reason to be mad), while in women it is seen as a personality defect (i.e., she is an angry person or just "out of control").

In 2015, a study was conducted using undergrads who were asked to be jurors for a real murder case. Other jurors were fictional computer creations. All but one of these made-up jurors were programmed to agree with the undergrad. The one was programmed to be the angry holdout. In some cases, the holdout was given a male persona and in others a female persona. The results were unequivocal:

---

73   Ibid.

the angry male holdouts got more respect while the angry women got less. The impact on the undergrads based on the sex of the angry dissenter was even more interesting. If the dissenter was male, the undergrads became less confident of their own judgment and were more likely to be swayed by his opinion. However, when the angry dissenter was a woman, participants became more adamant, digging their heels in to hold their original opinion. If she was angry and emotional, clearly, she did not deserve respect.[74]

When men and women are involved in a discussion and no designated leader is apparent, the men have higher status in the conversation, unless the conversation topic is one that involves stereotypically feminine expertise, like fashion or raising kids. Contrast this with the story below:[75]

"Perhaps the best way to understand the respect gap is to listen to those who have experienced both sides of it. Stanford biologist Ben Barnes, former chair of neurobiology, has degrees from MIT, Dartmouth, and Harvard. He is the leading expert on nerves called glia. Barnes was born as Barbara and transitioned at age forty-two. She excelled in math, but her guidance counselor suggested she go to a local college; she went to MIT anyway. When she was the only one able to solve a difficult problem, her professor accused her of cheating: "he told me my boyfriend must have solved it for

---

74 Ibid.
75 Ibid.

me." She lost out on a prestigious fellowship despite having published six papers, five more than the male student who received the post instead of her."

Shortly after he had transitioned, Barnes was presenting a paper to a group of renowned scientists at the Whitehead Institute for Biomedical Research in Cambridge Mass. A fellow scientist, unaware of his transition, confided to a colleague: "Ben Barnes' work is much better than his sister Barbara's." Barnes wrote about his experience in Nature magazine:

> "People treat me with more respect. My authority is not questioned as frequently, and he's not overlooked in conversations. I can even complete a whole sentence without being interrupted by a man," Barnes admits. "This is why women are not breaking into academic jobs at any appreciable rate. Not childcare, not family responsibilities, I have had this thought a million times, I am taken more seriously." [76]

In the story above, we have a clear case of a woman with incredible expertise. She, however, is not offered the gift of being accepted as an expert at face value because she was a woman. Now, how would you feel having already established your credibility as an expert only to find the people

---

76 Ibid.

were constantly second-guessing you? How would it feel to have to reestablish your credentials over and over again?

I have experienced this frustration on numerous occasions. Once, my boss came into my office and asked why I didn't have my engineering degree hanging on the wall. I was kind of scratching my head, wondering why he would ask me that. Then, he blurted out the rest of the story. The auditors had been reviewing some work I had verified. They asked: "How is this woman qualified to review this work?" "She has an engineering degree, of course" was the response. The retort was then "show it to me." I have always wondered: would that question have even been asked if I were a man?

Try being a woman and you'll know. Women constantly face the "prove it again" paradox where they must constantly reestablish their competency. Social scientists have analyzed this problem and determined that women must be two and half times more competent than a man to be viewed as his equal, which is part of why men get promoted based on their potential and women are promoted only after they have proven themselves.

I believe that this phenomenon is the reason so many women leave the tech industry after ten or twelve years—they simply get tired of proving themselves over and over again.

Another way to think about it is: women are presumed incompetent until they prove otherwise. Men are presumed competent from the start. Research summarized in Lipman's book concludes that when women do succeed, their success is attributed to either outside causes or luck, while men's success is attributed to their skill.

I started a meal preparation business with my husband, who is a fabulous chef. He had been cooking as a personal chef, and we wanted to try and offer his services to more clients. The business went really well until the 2008 financial crisis, which wiped out a lot of discretionary spending, especially in Silicon Valley. Just as we decided I needed to go back to corporate America, I got a call from one of my past bosses, who told me he was consulting with a company headquartered back east that wanted to open an office in San Jose. I interviewed with what looked like a fabulous team and was offered a job. My job description was to look at the existing technology of the company and the skills we were hiring and figure out how to penetrate this new market segment. In my spare time, I was to develop a technology roadmap and secure the development funding needed for technology development to further penetrate the market. Just my kind of job!

About nine months into the job, my boss called me into a one-on-one meeting. He sheepishly told me that when he hired me, he had not been too sure how I would work out. I had not been in the industry for a number of years and had three small children at home. However, based on my performance, he had negotiated a large raise for me outside of the normal salary adjustment process.

I have been ambivalent about this interaction since it happened. On the one hand, he proactively went out and secured the raise on his own. No easy feat, I'm sure. It would have been easy for anyone in that position to just let it slide until the annual review. From this perspective, I applaud his efforts.

But when I look back at how it got started, it was not right. I had not been in the industry for a number of years, that was true, but I had seventeen years of solid industry experience. I had also been in two additional industries for another seven years—experience that offered me a much broader horizon of experience to draw from, just what you'd need to penetrate new markets. No credit was offered for having started and run a business, as if that venture didn't count at all, perhaps because he didn't see it as "technical." What he said was: "You've been out of the workforce for a while." Then there was: "You've got three small kids." Well, yes, I did, and he knew that I delayed my start date to ensure I had time to find a solid full-time nanny so I would not have to worry about them while I was at work or when I traveled.

The real test in my mind was: would he have done the same thing to a man?

The answer is clearly not—and that is where the issue lies. Women are judged on performance, and men are judged on potential. We need to figure out how to remove this paradigm from corporate America. One of the first steps is to realize that we are applying inconsistent sex-based rules or yardsticks.

MISTAKES

What about mistakes, you might ask? Women's mistakes get noticed more and are remembered longer, according to Lipman.[77]

Women and men also have a different mindset about mistakes. When women are more knowledgeable than men, and men have already made a noticeable mistake, women still take the time to listen to the men. They still consider the men's input and allow the information to influence their opinions. In the opposite scenario, when a woman makes a mistake, the man seems to become more determined not to change his opinion. This reality means women's mistakes are more costly than men's, as valuable information may not get considered when a woman makes a mistake. Because of this phenomenon, women tend to think through every angle of a decision to ensure they continue to be taken seriously. According to Therese Huston, author of How Women Decide, this explains why women are more analytical and systematic in their thinking in the workplace:[78]

---

77 Ibid.
78 Huston, Therese. How Women Decide; What's True, What's Not, and What Strategies Spark the Best Choices. Mariner Books, 2016.

"I've found that when a man faces a hard decision, he has to think about making a judgment, but when a woman faces a hard decision, she has to think about making a judgment and also navigate being judged."

EMOTIONS

Are women more emotional than men? Perhaps we should consider that we all have the same capacity for emotion, but our society has dictated and hence trained men that their displays of emotion are unacceptable, especially at work. After all we all know the old adage, "big boys don't cry."

Let's back up a minute and take a look at what emotions do for us and why we have them. Emotions tell us what other people are feeling in the moment. Our senses evolved to be able to take a quick look at a person and size them up. At our most primitive selves, upon encountering another person, we quickly needed to decide whether the person was a friend or foe, which would dictate if we should approach them or run the other way.

Women do have an advantage, according to Helen Fisher, because:[79]

---

79 Fisher, Helen. *The First Sex; the Natural Talents of Women and How They are Changing the World*, Ballantine Books, 2000.

"Women are built for mindreading. Touch, hearing, smell, taste, vision: all of women's senses are in some respects, more finely tuned than those of men."

Based on your body posture and gestures, women can determine your mood. They even remember more details about people's physical surroundings that they use to interpret the social context of a situation.

Men are also quite capable of reading emotions. In a fascinating study, researchers discovered that men can read emotions just as well as women. The key here was that they do so only when the right expectations and motivation are involved, when they believe their cognitive ability (intelligence) is being tested. If you tell them empathy is being tested, forget it. However, test college-aged men and infer that their ability to read another person's emotions might result in more sex, and their scores dramatically improve.[80] Perhaps that means men just don't normally feel motivated to read emotions.

If you look at ten-year-old children, boys and girls express the same amount of anger. As puberty hits and testosterone rises, boys who are becoming men begin to mask their feelings, especially those of vulnerability and weakness. Instead of showing loneliness, fear, anxiety, or guilt, they invoke silence. Another mask they use is to make quips, jokes,

---

80 Ibid.

and offhand remarks instead of displaying their emotions. Some men become so good at masking emotions that they honestly have no idea how they actually feel.[81]

There is an intriguing explanation for men's ability to contain their emotions. Psychologists Guttman and Levenson believe that men's negative emotions trigger their autonomous nervous system, which can launch us into that fight or flight response. Once this system is aroused in men, they recover more slowly than women. Continuous stimulation of this system is harmful to our bodies. These psychologists think that men withdraw from conflict to avoid this emotional rollercoaster to preserve their health. The two hemispheres of the brain are less well-connected in men, which may allow them to better compartmentalize their emotions.[82]

Women are not so lucky and have to experience and live with their feelings. In fact, women's emotions can occasionally overtake them, spilling out with little warning. My boys frequently "check Mom for tears" at the end of a movie.

Lipman reviewed some blogs about women and tears and came up with this classic line:[83]

"A crying woman is every man's kryptonite."

---

81 Ibid.
82 Ibid.
83 Lipman, Joanne. That's What She Said: What Men Need to Know (And Women Need to Tell Them) About Working Together. Harper Collins Publishers, 2018.

Crying is one of the things that women do that completely disarms men and sends them running for the exits.

In 2010, Israeli scientists looked at the impact of women's tears on men, and their findings are intriguing. Women's tears cause men's testosterone levels to fall, which makes men feel like they are losing their edge. Most amazing is that, in this study, the men did not even see the tears; they only had the opportunity to smell them—powerful stuff![84]

Some believe that emotional tears protect us. Babies signal they are in need with tears. Later in life, tears signal that we may need help, and if we are in different environments, may signal others to back off and back down.

What many men fail to realize is that often when women cry in the office, they may be signaling something completely different. They are so angry or frustrated that they can no longer contain their emotions, and the tears start flowing. Frequently, they are not sad; they are absolutely furious. If we were men, this would be the emotional point when we slam our fist through a wall. But it's not acceptable for us to respond that way, so we inadvertently cry. Don't be confused: we are mad as hell.

If you really want to comfort a woman in tears at work, you need to bring out your empathy. Ask how she feels. Women are not looking for you to fix anything, change

---

84   Palca, Joe. "Smell That Sadness? Female Tears Turn Off Men". NPR, Jan 7, 2011.

anything, or even do anything, necessarily. Mostly, simply acknowledging their pain means a lot to them.

One of the things that amazes me is the different reactions men and women receive at work in response to tears.

"A man gets a standing ovation for crying because he's so sensitive, but a woman is shamed," according to film director Catherine Hardwicke.[85]

Several studies have indicated that having a daughter can make men more empathetic. Dr. Relly Nadler wrote the book Leading with Emotional Intelligence. He was educated as a clinical psychologist and has both a son and a daughter, so has experienced the impact a daughter can have on men's emotional capacity. "With my daughter, almost all our conversations are around relationships—what's going on with her friends and how she's feeling. With my son, it's usually about things—things he wants to buy, places he wants to go, things he wants to do," says Nadler. He continues:

"What we know about neuroscience is that emotions are contagious."

85 Lipman, Joanne. That's What She Said: What Men Need to Know (And Women Need to Tell Them) About Working Together. Harper Collins Publishers, 2018.

When you spend time with your daughters, you pick up on their emotions, which sensitizes you and makes you more attuned to their issues. Then, when you go into work, you take that with you and are capable of being more sensitive to women.[86]

If Nadler is right, you may not need to have a daughter to become more empathetic to women. You probably only need to spend time and have some deep discussions with women you care deeply about and respect for the effect to wear off on you.

HOW WELL DO WE JUDGE?

Throughout our lives, we do a lot of judging. We judge how smart people are, how good their work is, even what skills and resources we need to get a job done. So, how well do we make these judgments? Let's look at a few examples.

A study was performed using 1,700 biology students from the University of Washington. Male students were asked to identify peers with a strong understanding of the material. The researchers found that the students overwhelmingly picked other men. They concluded that, in the heads of the students, the female students would need to earn an A to be viewed as equal to the male students who had a B. This scene continues once they graduate. Female graduates are paid less than their male counterparts for the same entry-level jobs,

---

86 Evans, Lisa, "Why Men with Daughters May Be the Key to Closing the Gender Wage Gap," Fast Company, June 30, 2014.

partly due to the fact that the men are eight times more likely to negotiate their salary. As they climb the career ladder, the trend compounds. At every level, women are 15 percent less likely than men to be promoted. This statistic is from a joint survey by McKinsey and LeanIn that included 30,000 people over 118 companies.[87]

Another example of our judging ability comes from Frank Browning's The Fate of Gender:[88]

"It's not about gender; it's about what you've done. Another Silicon Valley Male responded with great self-confidence, 'in the technical world, it's 95% about what you know and what you've done. Then there are personality and odds and ends in there. In the technical world I haven't seen political positioning and posturing.'"

Compare this account to how women working in high tech saw their careers: "I had general expectations that is be evaluated on my merits alone and not necessarily my gender. That was the case earlier in my career," a senior level woman responded, but then, as she rose past middle management, she discovered how important it was to "be in the right place at the right time. Other factors definitely come into play the more senior you become. ... It becomes a club."

87 Lipman, Joanne. That's What She Said: What Men Need to Know (And Women Need to Tell Them) About Working Together. Harper Collins Publishers, 2018.
88 Browning, Frank. The Fate of Gender; Nature, Nurture, and the Human Future. Bloomsbury USA, 2016.

As Browning explains, "66.4% of the women saw the work groups inside their company as competitive with each other while only 47.1% of the men did."

Computer scientists at GitHub studied whose code was accepted and rejected and were shocked by what they found: women win. Women are better coders based on acceptance rates. It was an extraordinary conclusion—women are better coders than men.[89]

The study went a bit deeper with some very revealing results. Women only win if the judges do not know they are women. When their gender is revealed, the women's code gets rejected at a higher rate than that for men.

"In coding, as in life, women are marked down simply for being female," Lipman remarks.

I found this story in a fascinating book by Nilofer Merchant, The Power of Onlyness, and was intrigued by the message it delivered about how we judge what we need and then can be proven so wrong:[90]

The scientific community was stuck. Scientists knew they needed to understand how proteins within our bodies fold or,

---

89 Lipman, Joanne. That's What She Said: What Men Need to Know (And Women Need to Tell Them) About Working Together. Harper Collins Publishers, 2018.

90 Merchant, Nilofer. The Power of Onlyness; Make Your Wild Ideas Mighty Enough to Dent the World. Viking, 2017.

perhaps more importantly, how they misfold. It was believed that protein misfolding, or folding errors in proteins, were tied to diseases like Alzheimer's, AIDS, and amyotrophic lateral sclerosis (ALS), or Lou Gehrig's disease. Protein folding is a complicated cellular process that happens over a period of time and may have many intermediate steps before reaching its final three-dimensional structure.

A lot of research told the scientists that folding patterns could not be reduced to a set of rules either, so software algorithms were not going to help. What they required was human creativity and judgment. The traditional solution would be outrageously expensive, as it would involve hiring tons of experts to fold thousands of proteins. Thus researchers at University of Washington turned to crowdsourcing and created an online game called Foldit. Their initial game was designed to be used by Ph.D. students from around the world; the initial thought process was to capitalize on the students' desire to contribute and expand their skills and perhaps their credentials. However, the game required the contributors to understand detailed complexities of the underlying science. The impact was that they ended up setting the expertise bar so high that they inadvertently narrowed the potential participants to a small group who all had essentially the same scientific background.

Adrien Treuille from the University of Washington team realized that "What was more important was to let people learn concepts through trial and error so they could apply their own natural problem – solving skills. This got more people engaged, without lowering the quality of the results— at all."

One of the big problems, Treuille recognized, was jargon.

"Jargon is a shorthand, a kind of secret handshake that says you are either inside or outside our club."

Jargon is created to shorten communication between experts, but it turns out to isolate the experts at the same time. It can effectively shut out ideas from outside the expert community, because no one else can figure out what they are talking about. Most breakthroughs occur at the periphery of industries and are frequently sparked when experts encounter ideas or concepts outside their area of expertise.

The Foldit game was altered so a wider group of people could participate. Now new members could play games to learn the logic of how proteins fold. This new revision rewarded the players' individual progress. Unfortunately, the update caused a lot of duplicated effort driven by the players competing against each other instead of trying to reach the higher-level goal. It turns out simple problems can be solved by individuals. Complex problems, however, require combining different knowledge, frequently that which comes from perspectives based on different disciplines. So, the Foldit developers changed the game again to reward collaboration between players. The rewards were given out by players to other players who were helping others.

Once that change was made, the researchers monitored the resulting reward data and got another surprise: the players from top-tier schools were being awarded the most points. Fearing this outcome was erroneous, the researchers turned off the ability to see the other players' social status (including where they went to school). These adjustments to the system worked. In just ten days, the Foldit players were able to solve a puzzle that scientists had struggled with for fifteen years—they deciphered the structure of an AIDS virus. This breakthrough has already contributed to the development of new medicines.

The icing on the proverbial cake came when Foldit revealed the "winner." Who was the best protein folder in the world? I know you are expecting to hear the name of a preeminent scientist or someone from a top university in that field, because that's what we expect to hear and want to believe. It was Susanne Halitzgy. Her occupation was executive secretary at a rehab clinic in England. Her passion, however, was solving puzzles, Rubik's Cubes, and Sudoku. She had studied medicine early in her life but chose another career path due to the sexism she experienced.

If you think your team needs more expertise, more specialists, more fire power—you may need to think again. What makes a team great is diversity of thought. People who might approach problems differently. People with different backgrounds, assumptions, and experience.

How we judge is highly dependent not only on the judging criteria, but also on the judges selected and what we think we need in terms of expertise—and on any one of these we can and do go wrong, very easily.

PERCEPTIONS SUMMARY

We perceive our world in a variety of ways. This chapter includes a triad of lenses that affect our perceptions. Table 4 includes a summary of these perceptions.

The mindset perceptions derived from our use of language allow us to peer into others' minds and begin to understand their frame of reference. When we understand this, we can then interpret their behavior and statements in a different light.

Then we have the perception differences, which reflect our imperfections as humans and also show many of the tricks our brains use, without our knowledge, to view the world, make decisions, and try to set the world right.

Perceptions

Mindset Perceptions

See Table 3

Perception Differences	A Different Yardstick?
Estimations	Interruptions
Blind Spots	Respect Gap
Externalize/Internalize	Mistakes
Intuition	Emotions
Apologizing	Judging

Table 4: Perceptions: The Triad of Lenses We Use

CHAPTER 7

OUR DIFFERENCES: VALUES

———

Values reflect what is important to the way you live and work.

—ANONYMOUS

The third category to explore regarding our differences is what we value: what is important to us, both in our work and in our lives. It is true that our values change over our lifetimes, but they tend to change as our definition of success changes and evolves. For most people, what they value changes very slowly. We often establish several core values during our childhood, and the particular values we prioritize vary over our lifetime, producing a continuous balancing act that occurs in slow motion. Values do not always have hard boundaries, so it can be easy to slide over the edge of a boundary without realizing it.

Our values are important because they determine our priorities. They are how we tell if our life is turning out the way we want. When we are living our lives according to our values, we feel satisfied, content, satiated. When we are not, we feel significant cognitive dissonance, the phenomenon that occurs when we have conflicts between our attitudes, beliefs, and behaviors. Cognitive dissonance is one of the triggers that tells us we are not internally aligned.

Although we are rarely aware of it, we use our values in making day-to-day decisions about how we live our lives and do our work.

All people have different values; independent – and community-minded thinkers, however, tend to lean toward different ends of the spectrum on a variety of commonly held work-related values.

This chapter discusses some of these value dichotomies. The purpose of the discussion is to sensitize each of us to the fact that these continuums exist. It offers us the opportunity to consider how our values factor into our decision making and make us aware that others may be guided by different values in their choices of words, decisions, judgments, and life choices.

TASKS VS. RELATIONSHIPS

Two different leadership styles exist and differ in their orientations. The task-oriented style focuses on accomplishing the tasks and achieving the goals established by management. The independent-minded favor this approach. When this style is deployed, the focus is on the process of getting the work done, achieving the desired outcomes, and creating the right structures that offer efficient completion. Typically, the rewards are also structured around the accomplishment of the task-related goals. Taken to the extreme, this style puts task completion above all else. Some leaders may feel the need to micromanage to ensure deadlines are met. High turnover, especially of relationship-oriented employees, may occur with this style. Unless goals are defined across business groups, this approach may also lead to the development of "silo" mentality, where the accomplishment of a single group's goals is more important than the overall goals of the company.

The other end of this spectrum is the relationship orientation of leadership. This style focuses more on the professional and personal growth of the team rather than the timely completion of tasks. Positive feedback is used to reward relationship-building tasks that support the overall accomplishment of the tasks and goals. People who value relationships and community will be drawn to this leadership style as it fits well within their value system. The resulting flexibility of task accomplishment due to accommodating the needs and priorities of employees may result in lower productivity. It may also take longer to get things done.

The task vs. relationship dichotomy is shown in Figure 19.

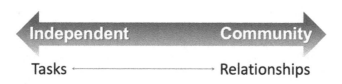

Figure 19: Tasks vs. Relationships

Both these styles have their pros and cons. What's most important is that you recognize that these approaches exist and make a conscious decision of which you want to use and to what degree and under what conditions you want to deploy it. Understanding your employees' natural style may help guide your selection of the most effective method for a given interaction.

ME VS. WE

The individual-minded have an individual or "me" focus, whereas community thinkers have a "we" focus. It is really a matter of whether you think of yourself as a "me" or a "we." If you listen carefully, you can "hear" another person's orientation in their conversation. Nothing is inherently wrong with either of these orientations. The problem arises when we interpret the conversations using our own lens, which can manifest in a couple of ways.

Let's examine what can happen during an interview. As the independent-minded answer interview questions, many of their statements will use "I," which clearly puts them in the driver's seat and in charge of their career and accomplishments. In the eyes of other independent-minded people, they are offered status because of these feats and are clearly in charge and independent based upon the language that they use.

Now, enter the community-minded interviewee. Their language includes the frequent use of "we," and they refer to the accomplishments of their team. To an independent-minded person, their language sounds odd—they are interviewing this person, not their team. "What have you done?" they want to know. But that is not how the community-minded think or how they talk. Additionally, they typically will not flaunt their accomplishments because they need to maintain that level playing field, which seems odd to the independent-minded, who have the expectation that, especially during an interview, interviewees should be pulling out all the stops to display their status from their previous jobs as an indicator of how great they will perform in this new position.

Note also that if we switch the roles and have an independent-minded person being interviewed by a community-minded person, we run into different but similar misinterpretations. The "I" language of the independent-minded can be misinterpreted as boasting or arrogance and demonstrate a lack of caring for others or for teamwork when interpreted through a community-minded person's lens. Figure 20 shows the me vs. we dichotomy.

Figure 20: Me vs. We

As you listen to people, pay attention to their "me" vs. "we" orientation. This distinction is especially important when you discover that you are on differing ends of the spectrum. Don't make a lot of assumptions about people based on the language they use. You may want to ask more specific questions around the area of teamwork and working independently. It can be too easy to misconstrue intent based simply on language.

HOW WE BOND

The independent-minded bond through banter. You can think of it as a friendly exchange of remarks that include an overtone of teasing; it can also include a lot of witty remarks and joking. Banter is a kind of light verbal play that seldom includes serious topics. It usually ends with everyone feeling a little bit better, at least among the independent-minded. When independent thinkers have worked together for a while, the joking may involve past work-related incidents, like "I remember when you...ha ha ha," where the remembrance may involve the recall of a potentially embarrassing incident. I often visualize banter as the gentle elbow nudge in the ribs. The purpose of banter is to build up relationships and get to know others a bit. During the banter, a bit of each person is revealed, and over the long term the independent-minded get to know each other with this ritual.

The community-minded bond in a completely different manner: by sharing deeply personal information, typically in the form of stories about themselves and others. These exchanges are usually in small intimate groups of just two to three people. The stories they tell communicate the values they hold. The more similar the values, the more deeply the bond that can develop. Even when the stories are about another person, the commentary or acceptance of the values exhibited share quite a bit about the person. The community-minded will also disclose minor secrets about themselves and often use self-deprecating humor, which tends to turn off the independent-minded, as this self-mockery is considered by them to be passive, a bit pathetic, and certainly not appropriate for business settings.[91]

Figure 21 shows the dichotomy of how we bond.

---

91   Fisher, Helen. *The First Sex; the Natural Talents of Women and How They are Changing the World*, Ballantine Books, 2000.

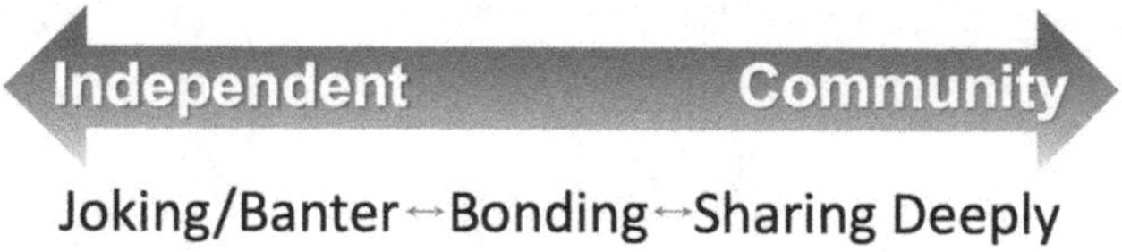

◄ Independent   Community ►

Joking/Banter ↔ Bonding ↔ Sharing Deeply

Figure 21: How We Bond

As I am sure you are aware, there is no "class" offered on how to bond with others. You can easily see that the ways the independent – and community-minded bond are on opposite ends of a spectrum, with the independent-minded focusing on lighthearted joking and the community-minded choosing to share deeply personal information.

Picture independent – and community-minded people attempting to bond with the other, each using their own preferred styles. The independent-minded person is being lighthearted and using witty teasing, while the community-minded one is trying to share something deep. I'm sure it's clear to you that these two mix like oil and water. This scenario is what often happens in the workplace. Picture this scene in the few minutes while people are assembling for a meeting.

Stuart and Tien enter the room laughing merrily as they have been bantering about what Julio had been wearing the night before at dinner: a lovely purple shirt. Andrea and Sarah are already in the conference room, quietly chatting about how difficult raising kids can be, especially when they're in middle school. Stuart makes a quippy remark about what Andrea is wearing, continuing to banter as he was with Tien. Andrea did not hear their previous conversation and becomes a little offended about the remark about her clothes. Sarah is a little perturbed about the interruption of her conversation with Andrea, as she had wanted to hear the outcome of the story about Andrea's seventh grader's first romantic encounter at the school dance.

Just then, the meeting gets called to order. Andrea is wondering what Stuart intended with his remark about her blouse. Sarah is thinking Stuart and Tien will never grow up and act like adults. Meanwhile, Stuart and Julio are now focusing in on the agenda; they have exchanged some banter with the two women and are ready to get to work. They have no idea that their remarks may have caused some angst for the community-minded. After all, they included them in their banter as soon as they entered the room.

SPEED VS. OUTCOME

As we learned earlier, the independent-minded's brains are wired for "perceive then act" connections, which may be why one of their priorities is on speed. They want to accomplish tasks quickly and efficiently. Check those tasks off the list.

The community-minded, while they love accomplishing things too, want to ensure that the outcome of the task is right. In this context, the outcome includes both the deliverables and how everyone feels after the project is complete. So, if the project is complete, but half the team feels like they've been beaten up the process, then the result is inadequate even if the deliverable was perfect.

The speed vs. outcome dichotomy is shown in Figure 22.

Figure 22: Speed vs. Outcome

Perhaps the best example for this divide is from my days of being a Cub Scout den leader, a role that entails meeting weekly with the scouts to do projects that expand their skills. Often, the scouts have never even tried the skill before, so they are not too good at it. For one project, they were going to build a simple wooden toolbox. They needed to transfer measurements onto the wood, cut out the pieces, then assemble the pieces using glue and nails. Most of these skills were completely new to many of them.

I constantly found myself asking some parents to put down the tools and let their scout pick them up. You see, the parents wanted their kids to end up with a nice-looking toolbox (the task). But our goal was to get the child to actually build it themselves (the outcome). The pride on their faces while they displayed their toolboxes (which were somewhat misshapen with ends that didn't quite line up) far surpassed anything you'd get from the kid with a perfect looking tool-box built by their parent. Part of the desired outcome here was building the skills, learning to use the tools, and taking pride in one's work.

Often, at work, we run into this mixing of desired out-comes. Do we want the perfect report in the shortest pos-sible time, or do we really want to give a new employee the opportunity to try preparing a report to see if that task is something they would want to do in the future?

RESULTS VS. CHALLENGES OVERCOME

Another dichotomy relies on the same twist of defini-tion as discussed above: achieving the desired results (think deliverables here) vs. the challenges that had to be overcome. Did you deliver what was asked of you? The answer really depends on who judges the definition of results. Both the independent – and community-minded understand the need to complete the deliverable. I expect they can agree on cri-teria to judge the quality of a deliverable. One of the big dif-ferences is that the community-minded also give themselves and others "points" based on the challenges that had to be overcome to complete the task. They might use this tactic because working with a particular group is difficult, it's the first time a task has been tried, or even because the timing itself complicates matters.

The results vs. challenges overcome dichotomy is shown in Figure 23.

Results ←————→ Challenges Overcome

Figure 23: Results vs. Challenges Overcome

This dichotomy is best illustrated by a story. At one point in my career, I was in charge of the group at GE that helped relicense nuclear power plants to a higher power level. Increasing the power level of a nuclear plant meant lots of money to our customers because they could generate more electricity. But we had to not only convince them the benefits outweighed the costs, but also determine the optimum power level based on their existing plant, which entailed figuring out what equipment would need to be upgraded and how much that would cost. One of the larger and more expensive pieces of equipment was the turbine. At some point, I was put in charge of trying to "get alignment" with our sister division that was responsible for upgrading that equipment.

On my first trip out, I discovered that this task was going to be much more challenging than I ever anticipated. First, our sister division was focused on other (read: much more important) objectives that had nothing to do with my project. Second, the people in that division had a completely different mindset about how to even approach the problem. Their approach was simple: "tell me the power level you want to achieve, and I will tell you the cost of the upgrade." We could not figure out the "optimized" power level without understanding the costs. What I wanted to get them to do was to create a rough idea of the costs for several different power levels. We could then add these costs to the cost curves we had generated for the other major components and determine an optimized power level to target.

The arguments were circular and endless. They would not "estimate" costs; they wanted to do a detailed and complete price analysis, including every single item. I was unable to get them to understand that we would be doing this for many, many plants, so the effort to do this process once would reap benefits for both divisions, over and over again. I really had two tasks. One was to get the cost estimates I needed immediately for a customer: the "result." The other was to affect a mindset change in this group, which clearly fell into the "challenges overcome" category. I succeeded at the first but failed at the second. The good news was that my boss was happy that we got what we needed for that particular customer. In his mind, I had succeeded. The bad news was that I felt that I had failed because I had not yet changed their mindset. We were no closer to having a working model to help clients optimize their power levels.

Whenever you are managing people, take the time to acknowledge the hurdles that have to be overcome to get the job done. To some, they may be more important and more challenging than completing the actual deliverable.

RISK: BOLD & DARING VS. CALCULATED

Quite a few studies have looked at gender differences in terms of risk-taking.

"People hesitate to take risks on women," Therese Huston reminds us. "Society sees risk taking as a man's world and that leads to a whole assortment of problems."[92]

Risks are an inevitable part of life, and men and women can approach them with very different mindsets.

"Our language makes it clear that it's almost the definition of masculine to embrace risk, and it's feminine to fear it," Huston points out.

Of course, risks are one aspect, but rewards must also factor into the equation if you really want to see a balanced picture—which is where it gets more interesting, particularly for businesses. Let's take a look at investment clubs. Lucky for us, some investment clubs are divided by gender. The National Association of Investors Corporation reported that women-only clubs reported a 21.3 percent average annual return. The men-only clubs made only a 15 percent annual return. Of those two groups, I know where I would put my money.[93]

---

92 Huston, Therese. How Women Decide; What's True, What's Not, and What Strategies Spark the Best Choices. Mariner Books, 2016.

93 Fisher, Helen. The First Sex; the Natural Talents of Women and How They are Changing the World, Ballantine Books, 2000.

Women are better investors than men. Sounds bold, doesn't it? Sally Krawcheck[94] is that kind of person, and from an investment perspective, she's an expert, having spent years on Wall Street. In her book, Own It, she says women are better investors than men, both at the individual and the professional level. The difference with Sallie is that she also shares the reason:

"Studies show women are inher-
ently more risk aware than men."

Risk-aware. Now that's an interesting concept. Additional studies have shown that when startups have women on their management team, they get better financial returns than those with only male leaders. Additionally, female CEOs are less likely to make value-destroying acquisitions, according to Sallie.

"Both men and women like novelty; both like variety; both like intense experiences. But boys and men seek thrills more regularly than women do," Helen Fisher informs us.[95]

In Fisher's book, The First Sex, she also credits psychologist Marvin Zuckerman for labeling these intense novel experiences as "sensation seeking." Perhaps the community-minded

---

94 Krawcheck, Sallie. Own It: The Power of Women at Work. Currency, 2017.
95 Fisher, Helen. *The First Sex; the Natural Talents of Women and How They are Changing the World*, Ballantine Books, 2000.

are able to stop short of this point, allowing them to evaluate the risk without getting caught up in the sensation part.

A few other interesting facts from Helen's book are worth repeating.

Female executives take on less debt than their male counterparts; they also make more profitable acquisitions. Companies with the most female board members outperform those with the least by almost every financial measure. Perhaps we should be calling these community-minded people "calculated risk takers," as they seem to be able to manage the risk-reward balance toward the reward spectrum.

Almost everyone knows the investment titan Warren Buffet. But did you know that LouAnn Lofton analyzed his investment style and wrote a book titled Warren Buffet Invests like a Girl? She made this statement because he only considers long-term investments and does not get involved in the crazy trading and knee-jerk panic reactions that can wipe out investors.[96]

Risk flavors our decisions; let's try to understand how it works. When we are in tense or stressful circumstances, the independent – and community-minded have opposite reactions.

---

96 Lipman, Joanne. That's What She Said: What Men Need to Know (And Women Need to Tell Them) About Working Together. Harper Collins Publishers, 2018.

"It's not that he's rational and she's not; it's that he's risk hungry and she's not," Huston explains.[97]

If you want judgment, balance, and insight in your decisions, you need both the independent – and community-minded in the room. Together they can offer the balance we need.

When we are stressed, people assume that women are just that way—stressed—all the time. For men, the assumption is they are just having a bad day. Stress hangs out with us twenty to forty minutes after the actual stressful experience. The cortisol that gets released when we are stressed lingers in our systems, keeping our bodies in a stressed condition.

Women when stressed are more likely to take the sure win over the higher risk. Men do the opposite, taking more chances. In fact, men seem to be risk-hungry when stressed. Under the wrong conditions, they may throw both caution and common sense out the door.

One study found that women became more strategic under stress, looking for smaller sure-fire successes, while men became more risk-seeking. Interestingly, cortisol has different reactions in men and women. A flood of cortisol makes women more risk-aware, while it makes men more

---

97 Huston, Therese. How Women Decide; What's True, What's Not, and What Strategies Spark the Best Choices. Mariner Books, 2016.

risk-seeking.[98] You should keep that in mind if you have to make a decision right after a stressful event.

The bold and daring vs. calculated risk dichotomy is shown in Figure 24.

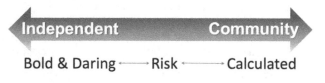

Figure 24 – Risk: Bold & Daring vs. Calculated

VALUES: SUMMARY

If we take all these characteristics together, we can create a framework around what we value that will help guide our understanding of our differences as shown in Table 5. You may see other dichotomies in your life, I would love to hear about them via www.YouCantFixWhatYouCantSee.com.

Again, neither side is right or wrong; they are both different and valid sets of values. I find that understanding these dichotomies helps me better relate to people who value things differently.

For example, I can banter with the independent-minded to bond, but I have to keep in mind that their teasing and light-hearted humor should not be construed as jabs at my

---

98 Ibid.

personality. They may be "picking on me" by bringing up the last faux-pas I made at a meeting, but their intent is not to cause harm—it's to make some light-hearted fun.

The other thing that we gain is a common language we can use to discuss our differences. By labeling these extremes of values, we can now have a way to talk about the differences.

Let's say you are in a meeting trying to get a proposal out to a client. The request the client sent you is a bit nebulous, and you are trying to figure out exactly what the client is trying to accomplish and why, so that what you offer will meet their needs. Several of the community-minded in the room are stuck on the outcome. "What are they trying to do?" they keep asking. No one has a good answer. While their concern is valid, you know you need to get the proposal together now or you won't get it to them in time, so you suggest that you have enough information to propose the work now without knowing the ultimate outcome. If you get your bid in, then at the next meeting you can try to figure out what you are ultimately trying to accomplish, which may help you with the next phase. But if we don't act quickly, your bid will not make the deadline and you will be excluded from the next meeting. So let's get going.

What We Value

Tasks ←——————→ Relationships
Me ←————————————→ We
Joking/Banter ⋯→ Bonding ←⋯ Sharing Deeply
Speed ←——————————→ Outcome
Results ←————→ Challenges Overcome
Bold & Daring ←→ Risk ←——→ Calculated

Table 5: What We Value

CHAPTER 8

WHAT WOMEN OFFER

———

*Everybody is a genius. But if you judge a fish by its ability to
climb a tree, it will live its whole life believing that it is stupid.*

—ALBERT EINSTEIN

FINANCIAL BENEFITS

Having a diverse workforce and being able to leverage
that diversity will make your company's financial performance soar. McKinsey has been analyzing and publishing
this data for several years. Its latest report, published in 2018,
uses company data from 2017. It looks at this data comparing
financial performance of those companies in the top quartile

for gender diversity on their executive teams with the companies in the fourth quartile. Here's what they found:[99]

21 percent more likely to experience above average profitability

33 percent more likely to outperform on Profitability (EBIT margin)

27 percent more likely to experience value creation (profit margin)

What company wouldn't want these financial advantages in today's business world? In fact, maybe the question we should all ask ourselves is: how much are you willing to invest to get this kind of improvement?

LEADERSHIP CAPABILITIES

A number of studies have examined leadership competencies in business. In a 2019 study published in Harvard Business Review[100], using data taken from thousands of 360-degree reviews, women outscored men on seventeen of nineteen leadership capabilities. Since this data is from 360-degree reviews, a good portion of the data must have

---

99 Hunt, Vivian; Prince, Sara; Dixon-Fyle, Sundiatu;, and Yee, Lareina; "Delivering through Diversity," McKinsey & Company, Jan 2018.

100 Zenger, Jack; and Folkman, Joseph; "Research: Women Score Higher than Men in Most Leadership Skills," Harvard Business Review, June 25, 2019.

come from men. The differences shown in Table 6 are not large, but they are statistically significant.

Leadership Capability	Women's percentile	Men's percentile
Takes initiative	56	48
Resilience	55	49
Practices self-development	55	50
Drives for results	54	49
Displays high integrity and honesty	54	49
Develops others	54	50
Inspires and motivates others	54	50
Bold leadership	53	50
Builds relationships	53	50
Champions change	53	50
Establishes stretch goals	53	50
Collaboration and teamwork	53	50
Connects to the outside world	52	50
Communicates powerfully and prolifically	52	51
Solves problems and analyzes issues	52	50
Leadership speed	52	51
Innovates	51	51
Technical or professional expertise	50	51
Develops strategic perspective	50	51

Table 6: Leadership Capabilities as Demonstrated by Women and Men[101]

---

101 Ibid.

This data is consistent with previously published data that indicated men are slightly better at strategic perspective and technical or professional expertise.

Based on this data, one would think that percentages of men and women in leadership positions should be much more balanced. Sadly, only 4.9 percent of Fortune 500 CEOs and 2 percent of the S&P 500 CEOs are women.

"Women are perceived by their managers — particularly their male managers — to be slightly more effective than men at every hierarchical level and in virtually every functional area of the organization. That includes the traditional male bastions of IT, operations, and legal," says Jack Zanger.

STRENGTHS

Women bring many strengths to the table, such as enhancing an organization's strength and driving profits higher while increasing engagement. Krawcheck shared six distinct traits that women possess that can improve an organization:[102]

- A healthy risk awareness
- The ability to see things holistically, which they use to manage complexity effectively

---

102 Krawcheck, Sallie. Own It: The Power of Women at Work. Currency, 2017.

- A focus on relationships
- The gift of a longer-term perspective
- A love of learning
- The drive for impact and meaning

To these you can add:

- Women seek advice and learn from it

I extracted this last one from Lipman's book, That's What She Said.[103] This quality is especially important as, more often than not, innovation is driven at the fringes of industry. So, the more people you have on the lookout for and willing to learn from what is happening in other industries, the more likely you will be able to spot and act on emerging trends before your competitors do. Also, here's your spoiler alert: look at the list above and compare it to the list of imperatives needed to create an authentic organization in the final chapter. I believe these strengths will become more and more important in the future.

DIVERSITY DRIVES INNOVATION

Sylvia Ann Hewitt did a study[104] examining the intersection of diversity and innovation. Her research included surveying 1,800 professionals and a review of forty case studies, along with several focus groups and interviews. In her study,

---

103 Lipman, Joanne. That's What She Said: What Men Need to Know (And Women Need to Tell Them) About Working Together. Harper Collins Publishers, 2018.
104 Hewlett, Sylvia Ann; Marshall, Melinda; Sherbin, Laura, "How Diversity Can Drive Innovation." Harvard Business Review, Dec 2013.

she identified two kinds of diversity: inherent and acquired. Inherent diversity is based on traits you are born with, like gender, ethnicity, and sexual orientation. Acquired diversity originated from traits you gain based on your life experiences. For example, acquired diversity might come from living in another country or doing nonprofit humanitarian work, anything that allows you to have in-depth knowledge. Companies that had leadership with both of these traits were shown to out-innovate and outperform other companies whose leaders did not have them. Hewitt found that employees at these companies were 45 percent likelier to report their firms market share grew and 70 percent likelier to report the firm was able to capture a new market.

Having these two dimensions of diversity in the leadership team creates an environment in which outside-the-box ideas actually get heard and consequently can be executed. As Hewitt explained:

> *"When minorities form a critical mass and leaders value differences, all employees can find senior people to go to bat for compelling ideas and can persuade those in charge of budgets to deploy resources to develop those ideas."*

Unfortunately, her research also revealed that 78 percent of the people surveyed worked at companies that don't have this depth of diversity in their leadership. At these companies, she found that various minorities were less likely than straight white men to win endorsement for their ideas with the following breakdown:

- Women were 20 percent less likely (than straight white men) to win endorsement for their ideas,
- People of color are 24 percent less likely, and
- LGBTQ people were 24% less likely.

This problem has a devastating impact on these companies' abilities to understand the unmet needs of markets.

"A team with a member who shares a client's ethnicity is 154% likelier than another team member to understand that client," Hewitt points out.

Her statement rings true for all kinds of diversity. Lipman shares a poignant example of this in her book That's What She Said.[105] The male executive running the Kotex business had been asked to explain their strategy at a board meeting. Afterward, one of the board members asked if perhaps he could get a woman to present the strategy. He looked at this org chart and realized that 81 percent of the top jobs were held by men. Lipman sums up the situation nicely in her book:

"If you've ever wondered why tampon commercials feature gleeful women twirling around in

---

105 Lipman, Joanne. That's What She Said: What Men Need to Know (And Women Need to Tell Them) About Working Together. Harper Collins Publishers, 2018.

all-white spandex — something no actual women having her actual period has ever willingly done — now you know," she writes.

Of course, you have to look at the acquired diversity aspect as well. What the study found is that six behaviors that come with acquired diversity are key to unlocking innovation:[106]

- Ensure that everyone is heard
- Make it safe to propose novel ideas
- Give team members decision-making authority
- Share credit for success
- Give actionable feedback
- Implement feedback from the team

Hewitt explains:

"Leaders who give diverse voices equal airtime are nearly twice as likely as others to unleash value-driving insights, and employees in a 'speak-up' culture are 3.5 times as likely to contribute their full innovative potential."

INNOVATION DRIVES DIVERSITY

Here is an interesting story that shows how you can create an upward spiral with diversity driving innovation and

---

106 Hewlett, Sylvia Ann; Marshall, Melinda; Sherbin, Laura, "How Diversity Can Drive Innovation." Harvard Business Review, Dec 2013.

then innovation driving even more diversity. In this example, the diversity driver is not gender, but race. In my mind, diversity in any form can drive great business results, which, in turn, can drive the understanding of the importance of diversity to bottom-line business results.

Julius Pryor was working with TAP Pharma (a partnership between Takeda and Abbot, now part of AbbVie), which had just released a drug for the treatment of prostate cancer. This new drug worked differently by suppressing testosterone that was indicated to cause the rapid growth of prostate cancer cells. It represented a new development in the treatment of prostate cancer.

According to the Prostate Cancer Foundation, black men are nearly 1.6 times more likely to develop prostate cancer and 2.4 times more likely to die of the disease. Furthermore, the recidivism rate for this cancer for black men was 60 percent. When Julius learned about these statistics, he immediately started discussions with the sales team, to ensure that their primary target was black physicians.

"I was shocked at the pushback I got from the team," Julius tells me. "They did not plan to target this demographic at all! The team came up with all kinds of excuses, like: 'this group does not pay their bills on time,' or 'the patients do not come back for treatment' (this drug required a once per month injection). I was floored. So, I went to the VP of Sales and said: 'Let's do a demonstration project. We can target just three African American physicians and see if we can get them to convert their patients over to this drug.' They set an arbitrary metric for success at conversion of just 30 percent of each physicians affected population."

Within the first six months, they converted not 30 nor 50 percent, but all of their affected patients over to the new drug from the three physicians in the demonstration pilot. It didn't stop there. Once the company saw the impressive results, the sales team got new directions. By twelve months, 20 percent of the total sales of this drug were coming through black physicians, even though they represented only 3 percent of the total physician demographic.

This development represented a big win, both for the patients and for the company. But the story doesn't end here. A year and a half later, the company began to use the same drug for women. It turns out that women with leiomyomas (fibroid tumors) would also benefit by this drug, which also suppressed estrogen. Black women were 80 to 90 percent likely to develop fibroids by age fifty (compared to 70 percent of white women). This new indication for the drug, along with the new demographic, added even more revenue to the company, with sales now measured in billions of dollars.

"The real kicker was the collateral benefits that happened at the company as a result of the demonstration project. Within three years, they tripled the number of minorities in the company," Julius explains. "That population went from 10 percent to 30 percent. The number of women in the company also rocketed from 10 percent to 30 percent. It was all because the leadership team could 'see' the impact this demographic had on the company. They 'got it' and acted accordingly, hiring more people who could effectively tap into these markets."

RESPONSIVENESS TO MARKETS & CLIENTS

It doesn't matter whether you look at the business to consumer market or the business to business market: women are now controlling a huge portion of the spending in these markets.

Women decide on 85 percent of consumer purchases.

As shown in Figure 25 below, women control 60 percent or more of the decision-making for many consumer categories.[107]

---

107 Yankelovich Monitor and Greenfield Online for Arnold's Women's Insight Team.

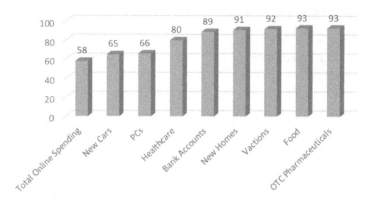

Consumer Spending Controlled by Women

Figure 25: Consumer Spending Decision by Women

Women are responsible for controlling $40 trillion in spending across the world in 2018.[108] That's a lot of spending power. You can ignore this reality only at your own peril.

Perhaps even more scary for the consumer companies that should be selling to these women is the following statistic:[109]

> *"91% of women feel that advertisers don't understand them."*

---

108 The Boston Consulting Group (BCG), "Women Want More: Updated Findings on the World's Largest, Fastest-Growing Market," Webinar Presentation, September 2013.

109 Yankelovich Monitor and Greenfield Online for Arnold's Women's Insight Team.

I don't know about you, but with women controlling that volume of consumer spending, I think I would start quickly trying to understand them. And who would be the best people to employ to drive that understanding? Well, women would probably be an excellent place to start.

***

Now, if you shift your focus over to the business to business market, you will find that:

Women are currently making 41 percent of company purchasing decisions.[110]

The question remains: is your company fully equipped to navigate this territory?

You will find some interesting dynamics in meetings where these business decisions are being made. When men and women meet to discuss a potential new contract, women view the meeting as a chance to explore options in collaboration with an expert resource. Men, on the other hand, may see the same meeting as a final step in the process and expect to be narrowing down and choosing options. These two very different intentions can cause a deal to fall apart before it even has a chance to coalesce.

---

110 Benko, Cathy and Pelster, Cathy. "How Women Decide," Harvard Business Review, Sept 2013.

Additionally, because of our differences, men might be inclined to end a meeting as soon as they get one good idea or a solution they connect with. Women, on the other hand, ask more questions and more rigorously explore options and vendors. With one person jumping up from the table to implement a solution and the other still in the exploratory phase, you can see again that the potential for a deal to fall apart is high. Unless, of course, your teams are gender-savvy and experienced at navigating our differences.

Women bring some other interesting strengths to the table around markets. Did you know that women are more likely to make referrals to others based on their positive experience? Based on one study, a woman would refer her financial adviser to others twenty-six times during her lifetime. That's a lot of referrals. Men would only make eleven referrals, less than half that of the women.[111] Your female clients can really amplify your reputation!

PREPARATION AND ADVICE

Frequently, as business leaders in today's world, we find ourselves facing new challenges where perhaps our knowledge is not as deep as we would prefer. Recognize that women have a willingness to both prepare for these situations and to seek outside advice.

---

111 Osterland, Andrew. "Female Clients more likely than men to make Referrals". Investment News, Apr 24, 2012.

According to Huston, when it comes to preparing ahead of time:[112]

"Men are comfortable winging it 65-70% of the time and only needed to prepare 30-35% of the time. Women believe they have to be prepared 80% of the time."

She also identified some interesting gender differences in terms of seeking advice: "Upon receiving a takeover bid, companies with more women on the board chose to hire the top M&A advisors. Where all male boards hired second tier advisors. Were the men extremely confident in their decision-making ability? They hired consultants, but it was a check the box, pro forma exercise. Also, those who hire the top tier (and pay top dollar), actually listen more closely to the recommendations."

So, if your company plans to "go where others have not gone before"—and what company doesn't?—you'd be much better off with a diverse mix of leaders throughout your organization, especially at the top.

---

112 Huston, Therese. How Women Decide; What's True, What's Not, and What Strategies Spark the Best Choices. Mariner Books, 2016.

CHAPTER 9

WHY CAN'T
THEY SEE IT?

———

*1 in 4 Americans think we'll colonize Mars before we see CEO
gender parity.*

—TAYLOR PITTMAN[113]

I feel strongly that one of the main reasons we have not
made as much progress as we'd like is that many people cannot see the problem.

The first step is to define The Problem.

———

113 Pitmann, Taylor. "1 In 4 Americans Think We'll Colonize Mars
Before We See CEO Gender Parity." HuffPost, May 17, 2016.

The problem is that women are a seriously underutilized asset in today's business world and businesses could use their skills to significantly enhance their performance.

What makes me think people don't see the problem? Because:

- Women are underrepresented in the workforce.
- Women are dramatically underrepresented in leadership as you move up the hierarchy.
- Those on the leadership team make up the "rules" and the current set of "rules"—especially the unwritten rules—cause women to be judged unfairly and by yardsticks calibrated years ago in alignment with male behavior preferences.
- The female talent pipeline for some careers is depressing (e.g., computer science); there is an especially large lack of women in STEM (science, technology, engineering, and math) careers. This gap is even more pronounced as both the pipeline is lacking and retention in these fields is dismal.
- The gender pay gap.

The list of items above is actually a short list of the symptoms that are a result of the problem. Here I have simply tried to capture the highlights of the symptoms. The list does go on.

The problem is caused by a combination of societal, linguistic, historical, cultural, and gendered norms that no longer work for women, men, families, or workplaces. I interviewed a lot of people for this book: experts, psychologists, industry leaders, media gurus, and women. The women's stories hit me the hardest.

They were all based on their experiences from work. These were women who loved their chosen field; that was clearly apparent when the interviews started. They got so excited at the beginning telling their stories as they began their advanced education and then started working. They were engaged and thrilled to be learning and working in their chosen field.

Then, as they progressed in their careers, their experiences began to change, which I heard as they relived them in our interviews. And I say "relived" because it was quite clear to me that in the retelling of their stories, they were reliving the pain, frustration, and angst of their pasts.

Many times, they were recounting experiences that had happened ten or twenty years before. Their memories were so vivid, even after so much time had passed, that tears came to their eyes. Mostly, they were tears of extreme frustration. Their efforts to deliver great work were being thwarted. They were not allowed to participate in a way that would make them successful, and they knew they were being blocked. They were blocked by the systems that had been created to serve men, but they didn't serve women well at all. The women I interviewed wanted to knock the barriers out of their way; they wanted to do more; they wanted to contribute. They were forced to slam into unmovable barriers, over and over again, until they reached such a place of exhaustion that they finally threw in the towel. Many had been swimming upstream, fighting the strong currents for so long that they were exhausted. Emotionally exhausted. Eventually, they got to the place of: *Is all this really worth it?*

Now, we've got to ask ourselves a question: who would design a workplace like this?

Based on this description, I'm sure few people would willingly and intentionally design this system. Yet this is exactly where we sit today. We arrived here through a combination of our history, our bodies, and our norms, but that does not mean we have to stay in this place.

The first step to escaping our current predicament is getting people to actually see the problem. Until this realization happens, we won't have enough momentum to move us forward. Inertia is a powerful force. It takes a lot more force to get an immobile object to move than it does to keep it moving. We urgently need people to "see" this problem so we can start some real movement and overcome it.

Three large groups of people seem to have more difficulty "seeing" the problem:

- Entry-level people
- People not in hierarchies
- Men

ENTRY-LEVEL

Entry-level people and those on the lower rungs of the totem pole often do not see a problem. This relative position in a company implies a time and place where people are "learning the ropes," figuring out their jobs, and trying to fit in. They are busy, encountering new challenges every day, and perhaps a bit overwhelmed yet still exhilarated about their new careers. They may not have enough experience yet to develop those intuitive detectors that signal to you that circumstances may not be quite as good as they seem. I personally spent several years in this state. It's like your very first trip to Disneyland when you still have pixie dust in your eyes. People who are new in their positions are so overwhelmed figuring out what their job is and how to do it that they may not have the bandwidth to recognize nuances in how they are being treated and how it might be different from how others are treated.

Many people, both men and women, described to me a slowly dawning realization that something was amiss. Typically, they start to see it as they progress upward in the organization. They realize that other people are being offered more opportunities, receiving promotions, and getting those choice assignments. It can take quite a while for people to figure this imbalance out. It can be subtle. It feels a lot like exclusion. Exclusion is tricky, because people are not taking things away from you; you are just not being offered opportunities. Spotting what's wrong is always easier than what's not there.

It's easy to understand why entry-level people can't see the problem. They are so busy trying to get grounded and understand their job that they don't have any extra capacity to pay attention to the more subtle signals.

NOT IN HIERARCHIES

Whole groups of people do not work in hierarchical organizations. Entrepreneurs, small businesses, and artisans are examples. Generally, these groupings of people are not in a position where others within their business are in a position to "judge" their worth.

Here we recognize that people not in hierarchies get most of their feedback directly from their clients They don't have intermediaries who rate their performance. Their clients support their businesses, and they thrive or they don't.

MEN – WHY CAN'T THEY SEE IT?

Clearly, many people do see it. For that fact I am grateful, because I sought out several of them to interview to see if they could help me identify how they learned to see it and how we can get the non-seeing to see.

Several themes emerged from my interviews about "Why Can't Men See It?" I first grouped these into two major categories based on the stages one would naturally progress through toward taking action. The first category focuses on Why They Can't See It and the second is What Prevents You From Engaging (once you see it).

In the first category, I further broke down the responses into the following components: Not in My Experience, Hard to See Your Privilege, Socialization and the Man Box, and Risk & Reward. I have also included a section in this grouping on How Women Can Help people to see it.

In this chapter, I have created a composite of what I heard in several interviews—and naturally, when I hear the same ideas from several people, I pull those to the top. I do, however, want to credit the thought leaders I spoke with, as they have a great deal of experience and have invested time and effort into trying to figure this out. The callout below includes a list of the thought leaders who contributed to this chapter of the book (clearly, it takes a village).

- David Smith, Ph.D., Associate Professor of Sociology at Naval War College & Co-Author of Athena Rising
- Declan Shavley, Executive Adviser and Board Member
- Joanne Lipman, Author of *That's What She Said*, CNBC Contributor, former Editor-in-Chief of *USA Today*
- Jay Pryor, Executive Adviser, Keynote Speaker, Founder Jay Pryor Consulting, LLC
- Julius Pryor III, Chair of the Board of Directors for Healthcare Innovation
- Avi Ben-Zeev, Psychology Professor and Diversity, Equity & Inclusion Speaker & Researcher
- Tasha Eurich, Author of *Insight*, Organizational Psychologist, Keynote Speaker

- Art Kleiner, Editor-in-Chief, PwC Global and Strategy + Business, co-Author "The Wise Advocate"
- Lori Eberly, Executive Coach, Keynote Speaker, Co-Author of "Fuckery"
- Jeffrey Tobias Halter, Gender Strategist, Founder of YWomen, Author of *WHY Women: The Leadership Imperative to Advancing Women and Engaging Men*
- Ray Arata, Founder of Better Man Conference, Keynote Speaker, Co-Founder of Inclusionary Leadership Group
- Ed Hoffman, Founder Knowledge Strategies, LLC; Senior Lecturer on Information & Knowledge Strategy, Columbia University; former Chief Knowledge Officer of NASA
- Bill Fitzsimmons, Retired EVP of Regulatory Affairs, Clinical and Research Quality Assurance at Astellas
- Marilyn Nagel, Chief Learning Officer of SAMI game, CEO of Watermark, and former Chief Diversity Officer Cisco

NOT IN MY EXPERIENCE

The strongest component that came through loud and clear from my interviews was that many men do not have the perspective to experience the working world through the eyes of a woman. They may have never experienced the things that women experience and so the experience is simply not there.

The analogy that comes to mind is scuba diving. If I am a diver and you have never been diving, I can explain, show you pictures and videos, and describe the underwater world ad infinitum, and you still may not be able to understand what it's really like: what it feels like, what it sounds like, how it makes you feel, etc. You can't really know what scuba diving is like until you actually go diving yourself.

A corollary can be made: does a fish know that it is in water? While I am not a fish, I expect they can only begin to understand what water means (and that they are in it) when they are removed from the water. You must experience both in order to "see" the difference. Most men have not had that opportunity to experience what it is like to be a woman in the working world.

It is a natural human tendency to believe that your experience is the same as everyone else's. I have often found that my childhood recollections do not match those of my siblings even though we were together experiencing the same situation.

IT IS HARD TO SEE YOUR OWN PRIVILEGE

Privilege is something that puts you at an advantage over others. Of course, the reverse of privilege is disadvantage or hardship. One of the best ways to get your head around privilege is to first consider what privileges you don't have.

So, grab a piece of paper and write down what privileges you do not have. For my list: I am not a white man, I am not rich, I do not have political power. Go ahead, make your list.

Now list the areas where you have privilege. Mine are: I am middle-class, I have three college degrees, I am white, I live in the United States. Your turn. In what areas do you have privilege? Make your list.

Now, go back into your history. Are there times in your life when you lacked some of the privileges that you now have? This recollection could also include a time when you were temporarily marginalized. Say, a man attending a women's conference. For me, there was a time when our family didn't have much money, didn't have a TV, etc. Now, just in case you are so lucky and have always had privilege, pick an acquaintance who is not so lucky and use their situation to prepare a list of privileges that they have gained but didn't use to have. Make your own list of privileges you don't have that have marginalized you.

How did your lack of privilege make you feel? Were there things you were denied or went without? This should include items where you have had to change your behavior because of lack of privilege. My kids gave me a great example of this the other day. We had been out in the sun for several hours and we were all hot, tired, and thirsty. We stopped in a store and I grabbed a bottle of water from the cooler and opened it and took a long delicious sip. As I stopped drinking, all three of my kids were staring at me and they said, "You can't do that,

Mom! You haven't paid for it yet." True, I was exerting my white middle-class adult privilege. It's obvious from looking at me that I can pay for it. Note that a kid does not have this privilege. Store clerks cannot "see" that they have money, so you can get easily get called out for doing what I did. How does that make you feel when that happens?

One of the real advantages of privilege is you don't have to think about it—at all. People without privilege always have to think about it. Can I speak up in this meeting? Can I walk into this building or room?

I had a very interesting experience. I went to high school in Alabama. We lived in the country and were close to the geographic line demarking whether you went to the county high school or the city high school. We were technically on the county high school side, so I went to the county high school for two years, but when it was time for me to take Algebra II, I was informed that the county high school would not be teaching it because not enough students wanted to take it. My mom thought, "No problem, we'll just enroll you in the city high school." But we were in for a big surprise: I didn't have this privilege! I couldn't just enroll in another school.

This transfer would not be simple. Apparently, many white students applied to attend the city high school because it had a higher percentage of white students. I actually had to attend a "hearing" to request my transfer. While there, I, a fifteen-year old kid, was accused of trying to transfer so that I could get into the "whiter school." I had to tell them it was not a matter of color, but one of math. I planned to go to college and get an engineering degree, and I really had to take Algebra II to get into college. They finally conceded only after they checked with the county high school and confirmed that they were not planning to teach the class. This memory was one of my first encounters with the bizarre constructs we create around privilege and race. It left an indelible impression on me.

There are innumerable people who are not afforded privilege. And, unlike me, they can't change it.

Hopefully, this story can help you see how hard it is to see a problem when you don't realize that you have privilege in that area. You typically don't see it until the privilege is removed.

SOCIALIZATION AND THE MAN BOX

All of us have been socialized into our roles, by our parents, schools, society, and workplaces. As our society changes, our socialization does not seem to keep up with the times.

I recently came across the "man box" concept.[114] The man box was drawn to epitomize the socialization of men. Society draws the box, then expects men to conform to the norms. Here's one definition of the man box. Men are supposed to be:

---

114 Greene, Mark; "The History of 'The Man Box.'" Medium, Jan 15.

- Powerful and dominating
- Fearless and in control
- Strong and emotionless
- Successful—in the boardroom, the bedroom, and on the ball field

In addition, women are objects, considered property, and have less value than men.

I highly encourage you to watch Tony Porters' TED Talk "A Call to Men." In this talk, he describes the man box concept in such vivid detail that I could never do it justice—just go watch it.

This box is so incredibly stifling for men and women that it amazes me that it persists. It restrains men from being human, exhibiting emotion, and being vulnerable. For women, it's equally confining. We'd actually prefer men that are human, faults and all, and we prefer to be equal partners with them as well. Women as property? Well, I think you can figure out how women feel about that. We all need to work together to free our society from these awful binding constraints.

Men have been socialized to treat women in a particular way. Our society and culture have long celebrated many traditions that twist the value of who we are as humans. Just look at the chivalry stories of old. The knight must rescue the damsel in distress. Men should either dominate or protect women. Here's an example of how that plays out in the workplace.

A male manager has an exciting overseas opportunity but doesn't offer it to the woman who recently had a baby. Our society has put forth a model that says she is weaker and should be looked after. Most men are just trying to do what they have been taught. The fact that they should offer that position to the woman with the new baby and let her decide may seem foreign to men. But, in reality, she may have a live-in nanny. Perhaps the foreign assignment is where her extended family lives. Maybe her partner is contemplating a career transition at the same time. You can't possibly guess her circumstances, so always give her the option to make her own choice.

Men have been and continue to be socialized to be strong, powerful, and tough, and we are pushing these traits down to the next generation. You cannot be vulnerable; it is a weakness. Emotions are considered soft and have no business being in the workplace. The man box requirements go on and on.

Honestly, most women I know would prefer more vulnerability, more emotion, more humanity from men. It is time to let our men out of this confining box and make it okay for them to be human, make mistakes, feel pain, express anguish, and seek solace. What we need are many men who are willing to be role models to break free of their box and demonstrate to others the rich rewards of living unconfined.

In my discussion with Avi Ben-Zeev, he made a very interesting point. Men continuously have to prove their manhood. Women don't ever have to prove their woman-hood, unless they don't have children. Women do, however, have to constantly prove their business value, as discussed in chapter five. Personally, I think it's time we call a truce: let's talk about how we each want to be, and free ourselves up to pursue loftier goals that don't require us to put anyone in a box.

It is vitally important that we talk about these things, bring them out of the unconscious operating mode where they have dwelled for so long, and start making conscious, visible, and verbalized choices. When we begin to verbalize these choices, we send a message to others that they too can make their own choices. The first part of making a decision is understanding that you do have a choice; it is yours to make.

RISK & REWARD

What will men get out of this? Why should they even pay enough attention to figure out if they want to engage? After all, our lives are busy, and we can't pay attention to everything.

Our gendered norms seem to have taken many of us off the deep end. I know many men who feel just as trapped as women by corporate norms and the invisible rules that bind us. I believe men have a tremendous amount to gain by engaging in these discussions.

The future of work is rapidly changing as we move toward a digital-knowledge-based workplace. Many forces beyond gender will shape the new face of work, and I think men want to engage and fully participate in the shaping of what work should look like going forward. After all, if men are not engaged in these discussions, how can you ensure that the outcome will also work for men?

Currently, around 20 percent of our employees are engaged at work, meaning 80 percent are either disengaged or actively disengaged (meaning they are doing more harm than good on the job). From a business perspective, it only makes sense to seek more engagement from employees. By opening up discussions that center around what people need and want at work, we can all benefit.

And the risk? Well, I suppose some would believe that even exploring gender differences like we have done in the "Our Differences" section of this book might put their job at risk. I guess that could be true. But if the company and leadership are that rigid, then I contend that your job is in jeopardy anyway. You just may not realize it yet!

More likely, by opening your mind up to gender differences and being willing to explore these, you are going to expand your thinking and the thinking of your team. You will discover new realities that will be good for your business. You can find new ways to engage your team members, which can be beneficial for business. Chapter eight included the advantages of having women be fully utilized assets in today's businesses.

There are men taking a big leap. These are the current stay-at-home dads. These brave souls are taking a huge leap out of the man box. In fact, everything they are doing is counter to the man box mantra. Are we applauding them? We should be. For whatever reason, they have taken on the role of child caretaker—and they are swimming upstream most of the time. My husband was a stay-at-home dad for a time. At first, none of the moms would even talk to him. It took a couple of years of him being around before they would finally engage in conversation. The dynamics of a parent participation school actually helped quite a bit, as there were training sessions and you worked in the classroom with all the children. That drove a shared common purpose that opened up conversations enough to develop some common ground for friendships to finally develop.

As a society, we should consider these brave souls our unicorns, forging new paths, learning new skills, and setting the stage for others to participate more fully in the overall family experience. These stay-at-home dads are trendsetters, and we should applaud their efforts and ask about their experiences.

HOW WOMEN CAN HELP

People are often afraid to be honest and truthful. If we are going to make progress in changing our behavior, we must have some frank conversations. Many things women do reflexively keep men in the dark. Often, women choose to stay silent and not share their perspective of a situation. In order for people to see the problems, we will have to talk about them—hopefully in a nondefensive manner. It is best to start with the assumption that whatever just occurred was not "intentional." It happened, let them know, and move on. Just a mention, never a lecture.

Share your feelings and encourage others to do the same. *When you say this, it makes me feel like that.* Don't keep this to yourself. You can't expect people to fix something they don't even know is there.

Avoid the damsel in distress and other fairytale scenarios. You don't want to trigger the chivalry card; it's been around for centuries and immediately drops us back into the Dark Ages.

Support men who are breaking out of the man box. Stay-at-home dads are one group of guys we should be applauding. Show them support and ask about their experience. Those dads in the office who are supporting their kids and families by showing up for their kids' activities need support too. And let's not forget that there are many men trying to support their parents and other elders; this is hard work and it takes both time, patience, and money. They all need to know by our actions that we believe the work they are doing in these areas is important.

Meet men where they are and recognize that they have not had a lot of practice with some of these things. You don't need to know how to talk about emotions if you're in the man box. It will take them some time to practice and learn. Recognize that doing so may be uncomfortable for them, even scary. Give them credit for trying, and if they mess up, don't bite their heads off. We want to meet their vulnerability with compassion and give them time and encouragement to figure out new behaviors that work for everyone.

WHAT KEEPS MEN FROM ENGAGING

Just because people can see a problem does not mean they will leap into action to solve it. A lot of considerations go into what goals we prioritize to pursue. Seeing it, of course, is the first step, but many possible roadblocks can affect our motivation to pursue solutions. This section outlines the two categories that leapt out based on my interviews around the question, "What keeps men from engaging?" These were conversations that followed the "Why They Can't See It" discussions and start with the presumption that they see the problem; now what keeps them from taking action?

IT'S NOT MY PROBLEM

"Sure, women have a problem at work, but it's not my problem. This is a problem for women."

This problem was created by our collective society. For too long, it has been described as an issue for women to fix. This is a business problem, and businesses need to actively work on the solution. Those that initiate the changes first will be the first to reap the rewards. So, you have to ask yourself:

"Do you want to be in the driver's seat on this issue, or do you want to be left reacting while others take the lead?"

I find many people also approach this problem with a zero-sum game philosophy, meaning that they believe that by supporting women in the workplace, men will lose out. Clearly, leading the charge of supporting women at work is a valiant effort, and no doubt it will take courage. But it will not result in the loss of status for men. I believe it will result in "freeing" men from the man box—a liberation that allows men more flexibility in their own work-life choices. Supporting women in the workplace will result in an expansion of the possibilities for your business, which in turn allows for growth for all. More importantly, when we combine the strengths of men and women, we can open up the floodgates of innovation. Working together, we have the potential to see and implement new possibilities that we cannot see on our own. I view it as a way to enhance business growth, open up new markets, and better serve existing markets. It's not a competition; it's a collaborative endeavor where bringing together different views can open up a world of possibilities.

FEAR

Fear is an important built-in response to protect us from physical and emotional danger. Once you understand the danger of a saber-toothed tiger, on your next encounter fear will prepare you for fight or flight. It triggers both a physical and emotional change in the body that can be rather uncomfortable. It usually takes quite some time for your body and mind to return to their normal state after a fear trigger (anyone who has been in traffic accident can attest to the time it takes to calm back down and get your head on straight). While the flight, fight, or freeze response is activated, you are hyper-alert for danger. It is not good for your body or mind to remain in the fear state.

I believe very few men fear women from a physical perspective. So it is primarily an emotional reaction, although the body does not discriminate based on the reason. Many fears can surface between men and women in the workplace. As we've discussed in earlier chapters, men and women are often different in how they respond. I think it is fair to say that men are more comfortable with other men, precisely because they can anticipate how they will respond. But when men respond to women, they face a higher likelihood of something unexpected happening. Many men fear that they will say or do the wrong thing around women. They fear "getting it wrong." This fear is not unfounded; it is usually based on the fact that it has happened before.

As Lipman has noted, "The problem can be exacerbated when these men become bosses. In one survey, 79 percent of male supervisors reported worrying about giving women candid feedback, and said they felt they had to provide guidance carefully and indirectly. The irony is that by self-censoring, the men don't give women the feedback necessary for the women to advance."[115]

Imagine this scenario: Several people are in a meeting brainstorming solutions to a problem. Ben is writing down ideas on the whiteboard while the team members call out their ideas. Sara brings up an idea, but Ben doesn't write it down. He doesn't see what it has to do with the problem they are trying to solve. This happens five or six times over the course of the meeting. Sara never says a thing when Ben doesn't write down her idea. She doesn't call out that he isn't writing her ideas down. And she doesn't get a chance to clarify how what she said related to the problem. Every time Ben ignores her ideas, she gets a little more miffed. By the end of the meeting, Sara is no longer contributing and is mad but still hasn't said anything. As she walks out the door, Ben thanks her for her participation, as he does for all participants. "Yeah right," she says sarcastically as she exits the meeting room.

At this point, Ben suddenly realizes Sara is angry, but he has no idea why. He stops by her office a little while later to try and figure out what is wrong. She gets up, tells him that he's a jerk, and storms out. At this point, he knows she is mad, and it is directed at him, but he still has no idea what he has done. In Sara's mind, Ben knows exactly what he did,

---

115 Lipman, Joanne. *That's What She Said: What Men and Women Need to Know About Working Together.* HarperCollins, 2018.

and she is sure he did it intentionally, so there is no reason for her to explain it to him.

This kind of situation happens a lot in our workplaces. Ben knows he did something wrong, but he has no idea what it was. He even tried to talk to Sara, but she wasn't having any of that, so he gives up, concludes that women are too emotional, and you just can't predict what might set them off. *Better be more careful around them or I might do something wrong again*, he thinks.

Men avoid what makes them uncomfortable. Certainly, in the scenario above, Ben became very uncomfortable at the end and never did understand what happened. He will avoid further encounters, fearing he will again be accused of doing something wrong without actually knowing what it is. Can you blame him?

This scenario could have gone quite differently. Had Sara asked why Ben wasn't writing down her ideas, perhaps he could have said he didn't see how they related to the problem they were solving. Then she could have clarified and explained how they did. Alternatively, Ben could have noticed that Sara was offering fewer ideas as the meeting progressed and asked her why, starting a conversation that could have brought out valuable information.

Men encounter other fears in the workplace as well, one of which is the fear of being teased or chastised by other men. Typically, this might occur if you break the man code, part of which is to "avoid all things feminine." This perceived breach may result in a loss of status and may generate some backlash from other men. What can you do? Take a stance. If you get teased or chastised, say why you chose your course in a way that might actually convince other men to listen. I choose to support the idea that we all contribute and our contributions may take very different forms. Then you can add your specifics:

"I choose to support her efforts by..."

"I choose to not demean women, even in private, because..."

"I choose to..."

More people piping up with the "why"s behind their actions can free others up to follow in their footsteps—this process is how change has always taken off.

Another huge fear concerns many men not exactly being sure of the rules for a cross-gender relationship at work. They may know how to be romantic with a woman, and they know how to be with the guys, but what are the rules for a work relationship with a woman? I was initially surprised by this fear but quickly realized it is undefined territory. Are you supposed to hold open doors for your work mates? Is it okay to ask a woman out for a beer, just like you would with the guys? How do you get to know them better?

What are the rules?

I believe that here we need to be straightforward and ask. What is wrong with saying, "Hey, we're going to be working together and I thought it would be good to get to know each other a little better. I want you to be comfortable, would it be better to grab a beer after work or maybe get together for lunch?" All you really need to do is get the conversation started, which might even be something you suggest for a team that will be working together. When you get to know your coworkers better, work goes more smoothly.

Another deep-seated fear emerged from my interviews: emotions. If you are going to talk about differences, then you are going to inevitably end up talking about "those squishy things," like emotions. Some men don't feel they have the skills to have this conversation. For years, they have been in the man box, and emotions are never invited there. Except anger—that's really the only emotion you are allowed. You're even encouraged to express it to demonstrate your power. But to discuss emotions? Well, that's something completely different. Men are quite capable of learning to discuss emotions, but we need to recognize that they will more than likely be on a learning curve. Let's choose to support their growth and be patient while they learn.

I would be remiss if I didn't mention the #MeToo movement, which started its viral spread in the fall of 2017. Technically, this movement was started to give people a sense of the magnitude of sexual harassment and sexual assault, especially in the workplace, which is a different topic than what this book is about. But the two topics often become intertwined as they both involve men and women in the workplace.

While I am glad some overripe bad apples get ousted, I fear the #MeToo movement is driving men to retreat and hide—the exact opposite of what we need to happen. Fear is a powerful force. But honestly, sexual harassment and assault have been ignored for too long. A new line has been drawn in the sand, and it's not going to be okay going forward.

However, many men feel like the rules have all changed, but they don't know what the new ones are. This outlook may sound crazy, but it never hurts to ask. Talking is better than retreating, and you might discover something interesting. Women should welcome these discussions and be open to discussing boundaries, just so everyone is on the same page. Opening these conversations will take some practice on both sides. It's really okay if we all learn together.

"The evidence shows that when men are deliberately engaged in gender inclusion programs, 96% of organizations see progress — compared to only 30% of organizations where men are not engaged," according to David Smith and Brad Johnson.[116]

This chapter has included a lot of information about what the problem is and why people can't see it. It's a complex situation involving many dynamics that, for the most part, people have been reluctant to discuss. We have reviewed many

116 Johnson, W. Brad and Smith, David G. "How Men Can Become Better Allies to Women." Harvard Business Review, Oct 18, 2018.

of the barriers that prevent men and women from seeing this system as a problem. We took a step further and looked at what prevents people from taking action once they see the problem. I really want to thank the people who took the time to share with me their perspectives and stories. This topic is not easy for any of us. Many suggestions were made on how to deal with certain aspects. One of the big themes in this chapter is that we are walking a new path and we can shorten and smooth out our route if we are willing to be vulnerable and discuss what is happening in an open and honest way. Everyone has a role in making this work.

CHAPTER 10

WHAT YOU CAN DO

Our potential is the one thing. What we do with it is quite another.

—ANGELA DUCKWORTH, GRIT AUTHOR[117]

Melinda Gates, in her book *The Moment of Lift*,[118] shares her revelation that came from a conversation with a mother of a newborn who had delivered the baby in a new clinic funded by the Sure Start Program. The interaction starts out with the new mom, Mina, reflecting on her successful birth and being able to bond with the child immediately. Mina

---

117 Duckworth, Angela. *Grit: The Power of Passion and Voice of Perseverance*, Scribner, 2018.
118 Gates, Melinda. *The Moment of Lift: How Empowering Women Changes the World*. Flatiron Books, 2019.

expressed appreciation of the program and how it helped her tremendously.

However, as Melinda asked her if she planned to have additional children, the conversation took a dark turn. Mina told Melinda that she and her husband were so poor that she was not sure how she could feed the two kids she now had. Then Mina said, "I have no hopes for this child's future at all" while looking at the newborn she held in her arms. "My only hope, if you'll take him home with you." Mina held the infant up, offering him to Melinda. This moment was a turning point for Melinda Gates; it was when she realized that all the prenatal, delivery, and post-partum care that her foundation was offering were never going to solve this woman's problem. What these women desperately needed was the ability to control the number and timing of their children. Melinda did a major pivot and started focusing the work of her Foundation on family planning.

The time has come for a major pivot on how we perceive the workplace.

The workplace is a societal construct that has evolved as technology has changed how we work and live. We have evolved from hunter-gatherers to the height of the Industrial Revolution, and now we're in the Digital Age with the Knowledge Era driving our economy. Yet our management practices seem to be firmly welded to the Industrial Revolution era. It is well past time to move forward in this regard. But how?

The model of what currently happens in the workplace is shown in Figure 26. We each start with our own secret decoder of how the world works. Then we run into problems because we don't all think alike. Our communication skills break down, leaving us unable to have the conversations we need to have. Frequently, someone assumes malicious intent in the situation. At this point, we arrive at an impasse, often with someone thinking, *I'm right and they're wrong.*

We don't think alike
Communication breaks down
Apply Mal-Intent

Impasse or
Right vs. Wrong

Figure 26: Current Workplace Model

In this chapter, I outline the seemingly simple steps needed to move forward. I say "seemingly simple," but the hard fact is that to progress, we need to change our gendered mindsets. I contend that these mindsets have been holding us back all along. These mindsets reside in each of us and in our societies in general. Our mindsets have been used to define the "rules of business," and the two have become so intertwined that we now can't really say which came first.

RECOGNIZE THIS IS A SOCIETAL PROBLEM

The first step is to recognize that this problem is societal. We have created it, and we are the only ones who can fix it. As a societal problem, we need to tackle it differently. It will take a group effort to change it. When we elevate it to a problem of society, then we must realize that this issue is:

- Not a Women's Problem
- Not a Men's Problem
- Not a Workplace Problem
- Not a Home Problem

Since it took all of us to get into this mess, it's going to take all of us to change it. You should note that I've added "Home" into the equation here. In order for all of us to flourish at what we do; we must include what happens in our homes as a critical piece of the puzzle. Often this part gets left out, but as a society, we have placed expectations about our roles not only at work, but also on the home and family front. Consequently, we must include what happens at home as part of what may need to change.

When we reframe this as a societal problem, several things happen:

- We all become responsible for fixing it.
- We see it as a "Systems Problem"—which means we can use some design thinking techniques to analyze and solve it. It also means there are many variables involved: individuals, couples, families, homes, companies, professional organizations. We need to factor all of these into our solutions.
- It also means it's nobody's "fault"; we need to move forward together.
- We need to open the fixes to a much wider range of solutions that will give us the flexibility to adopt not just new gender mindsets, but also new mindsets about work and home.

As an engineer, I know you cannot solve an over-constrained problem unless you're willing to relax some of the constraints. Certainly, we will need to do a lot of this along this journey. We really need to rethink how we live and work so that our work and our lives can be more integrated.

There's a first step each and every one of us needs to take. No matter where you are in this journey called life, we can only actively change ourselves. Yet, in the act of changing and becoming a more effective person, we also inspire those

around us to examine their own beliefs and start the change
process for themselves.

IT'S ALL ABOUT YOU – SEVEN STEP MODEL FOR LEVERAGING DIFFERENCES

Ama and Stephanie Marston's book *Type R: Transformative Resilience for Thriving in a Turbulent World*[119] shares a lot about the resilience we need to have to not just survive but thrive in our current world of constant, ever-faster spinning change. They offer a good summary of the challenge that each of us faces:

"We carry around an internal map of the world—a map of our professional and personal landscape and of our social, emotional, economic, or political terrain," Ama Marston explains. "In the same way we update maps to reflect a changing world, we have to update our understanding of ourselves, the situations we encounter, our surroundings, and the world we live in. If change or adversity transforms our personal or professional landscape, figuratively or literally, we have to relearn this territory—assess opportunities, risks, allies, available resources, and tools needed to not only survive but also prosper."

Yup—it is up to us to update our beliefs. Admittedly, this imperative rarely hits anyone's to-do list. Honestly, have you

---

119 Marston, Ama and Marston, Stephanie. *Type R: Transformative Resilience for Thriving in a Turbulent World*. PublicAffairs, 2018.

ever put "update my beliefs about xxx" on your to-do list? I know that I haven't, but we all should.

The adage "you can't teach an old dog new tricks" was used frequently when I was a kid, mainly to explain why people kept their favored and ingrained behaviors. It was also rooted in the current thinking of that era, where all your "learning" happened when you were young, and once you were an adult your brain was "fixed." As you've read throughout this book, science has debunked all these sayings as the myths they truly are. Science is an amazing eye-opener, and the ever-expanding era of neuroscience is certainly opening our minds in many ways. We have developed many tools to reach inside our minds in an attempt to see what is happening there. I believe we are just at the beginning of our understanding and expect that what we have learned thus far is just the tip of a very large iceberg. We all have a lot to learn, and as we do we will constantly need to update our beliefs to reflect our current reality.

So How Do We Go About Doing This?

1. **Explore your own and others' perceptions, values, and ways of processing information**

Each time you make a decision, ask yourself, *What am I assuming in reaching this conclusion, what paradigms are embedded in my response, and are they still true?* Then go validate or adjust your assumptions before you move forward.

Use the tables and information in the "Our Differences" section and think about where you are operating on a given spectrum and where others seem to be. Ask questions about the assumptions people are making, to bring the assumptions to the surface to be validated or modified.

Ask the question "What are you trying to achieve?" when people add criteria and qualifiers and you are not sure why they are adding them.

If people make statements in meetings and you are having trouble understanding the relevance to the topic at hand, ask about it by saying something like: "I'm having trouble connecting this to our discussion, can you please help me understand the relevance."

2. **Learn**

"Education is what other people do to you. Learning is what you do to yourself," author Joi Ito[120] writes.

Way back in the first chapter, I asked you to keep a list of things that spark your curiosity, things you want to learn more about, and even anomalies you encounter in life, like how the person down the hall has the uncanny ability to irritate you. Now is the time to pull out that list. If necessary, just take a few minutes to jot down some of these items now. These are things you are curious about, things you want to understand better, or questions like: *why do these things irritate me?*

---

120 Ito, Joi and Howe, Jeff. *Whiplash: How to Survive Our Faster Future.* Grand Central Publishing, 2016.

Now take your list and prioritize which you want to tackle first. Take the time to plan your learning, just like you would execute your to-do list. Now add these to that list. Set your own goals and then make sure you accomplish them. Add them to your to-do list and start checking them off.

Pick some areas that are interesting to you, like pay equity. Go learn about it, and start asking, *Why? Why does this happen? Has my company even done a pay equity evaluation to see where we are? Do we even know? What are we doing about this?* There are a lot of areas you can explore: How are growth assignments doled out at your company? How are promotions awarded? As part of this activity, you may identify people you want to talk with about some of your items. Go ahead and set up a time to have that discussion.

I contend that when each of us establishes and takes our personal learning plan seriously, we can start the change process. And have some fun along the way, too. After all, life is really just one big learning lab. At the next meeting you attend, listen intently and monitor how many people interrupt each other. Is it the same person doing the interrupting? Who is being interrupted? Announce what you learned at the end of the meeting and ask, "What should we do about this?"

3. Assess your situation at home

Look at the situation you have set up for yourself at home. Scrutinize the time you and your partner spend on home care and childcare. Is it equitable? What does your partner think? How many hours do you each spend on these tasks?

Is this balanced with the time spent at work, or are there adjustments needed? If you have one person clocking in at sixty hours and the other at a hundred, you probably need to make some adjustments.

While you are at it, take a look at how your family makes decisions. Is it equitable? Does it work for everyone involved? I have found that people who engage in planning are usually more satisfied with the outcome than those who don't actively contribute to the plan.

Vow to correct the deficiencies you identify. Note the specifics you are going to change and the date you will start implementing Ito, Joi and Howe, Jeff. *Whiplash: How to Survive Our Faster Future.* Grand Central Publishing, 2016.

them. Then set a date on which you will agree to reevaluate the situation and see if it is actually working. Make adjustments and keep moving forward.

4. Talk about your journey

Pick some areas to explore and let others know the journey you are on and why you embarked on it. These are not your typical office conversations, and they will bring you some rich experiences. We will all need to practice to learn the language to discuss these topics that are rarely discussed now. Use what you find out as talking points. For example, you may have started out being curious about why your product managers must have a computer science degree, but then you found out that many successful product managers (at your competitors and elsewhere) have other degrees. Maybe you should lobby to change the company protocol. Share with others what you are discovering and where you are on your journey.

5. Ask for help

When you ask for help, you are both inviting others in to explore the problem with you and admitting that you too have some things to learn. You will be surprised by the number of people willing to offer you a hand, if you are earnest in your request and in particular your quest for improved understanding. One of the most important parts of this journey may be to expose your vulnerability to others. When you do so, you invite others to join you in a much more profound way. It signals to others that you are embarking on a path where you do not have all the answers, and that part of the journey will be to have the team both identify the questions and seek the answers as part of the quest.

As we enter the digital and knowledge economy, we already know some key attributes that will be important. This, of course, is the age of data, driven by our growing ability to manipulate massive quantities and apply artificial intelligence to extract trends that the human brain may not be capable of seeing. The promise is huge. This trend is highlighted everywhere, but it frequently overshadows (or overruns) a second component that may be even more important.

How do you capture the human spirit? How do you engage the hearts of your teams, so they offer their 120 percent, because they are committed to the cause and understand that they are changing the world for the better (like Margaret Sanger)? Over and over again, this force has proven to be more powerful than decades of technological advancements.

Renée Mauborgne and W. Chan Kim, authors of *Blue Ocean Shift*,[121] are some of the first to have recognized this need and have built it into their process. Blue Ocean Shift is a process of exploration to identify and tap into markets you are currently not serving. This process combines two key elements. The first is a roadmap that includes processes and frameworks designed to help people create the space to facilitate learning about their markets. The second element is how to add the human spirit into the process, to really engage people who care deeply about an issue and want the world to work differently in this regard.

The Malaysian government was facing massive overcrowding in its prisons and a recidivism rate through the roof. It applied the Blue Ocean Shift process to challenge the fundamental assumptions about incarceration and brought together top leaders, like the prime ministers and high-level civil servants including those from the nation's security forces. Through its discovery process the government came to the following realizations:

- Not all people in prison need to be there, as the vast majority were incarcerated for petty crimes.

121 Kim, W. Chan and Mauborgne, Renée. *Blue Ocean Shift: Beyond Competing – Proven Steps to Inspire Confidence and Seize New Growth*. Hachette Books, 2017.

- Military bases around the country had idle land and a robust security infrastructure to protect the bases.
- Prison officials are good at confinement and high security, but not rehabilitation.
- Other ministries, like those in agriculture and education, have great vocational training.

Once the ministry officials looked beyond their own walls, they jointly created the Community Rehabilitation Program (CRP) for people who had committed petty crimes. Housed on military bases, the inmates learn critical skills and earn money through the sale of the products they make. The families were encouraged to visit often, and the officials created areas where visitors could actually interact with the inmates without the plexiglass walls. This change served to remind the inmates that they mattered to their families. The amazing results speak for themselves. The inmates learn new skills they can use to earn a living when they return to their families and homes. Just in the first few years, the government was able to achieve a 90 percent drop in the recidivism rate. The CRP centers are 85 percent cheaper to build and 58 percent cheaper to run than prisons.

The prime ministers from a variety of areas came together to understand the problem and create a novel solution. They were committed to finding a solution that worked, and they did this collaboratively across the ministries so that they all understood what they were trying to achieve and why it would work. The officials were totally committed to the concept before the first CRP was built.

What Kim and Mauborgne realized while creating their process was that, when people are sent reports, they don't realize what they know and don't know. Worse, they conclude that they understand, even when they really don't. When you actually have to dive in and roll up your sleeves, you value what you have learned because you have had to struggle to achieve it. It makes a huge difference, especially in the outcomes.

> "Making people discover firsthand that what they know — and don't know — is key to getting them to internalize and value what they learn," Kim and Mauborgne point out.

This fact is precisely why having a person or organization dedicated to diversity and inclusion within the company has not produced the results we all hoped to see. The leadership team has effectively delegated their responsibility away. What's worse, they also seem to have delegated their responsibility to learn away at the same time. What you need is a fundamental understanding to occur at the top of the company, so you can build the confidence needed to create and execute your diversity strategy. This will also provide the guiding light on how to build your strategy.

6. Help others "see" the issue

As I've said earlier, many people simply do not "see" the gender divide. The first step for all is to get everyone to "see" it, understand the ways it is holding us all back, and commit to supporting the eye-opening journey forward. So how do we go about doing that?

All the items that precede this one will help you set the stage. They will give you the background and some of the language that will be useful in talking with others about what you see. Then, start talking and asking others what they see. Approach these conversations with curiosity—you are trying to learn more, after all.

Marilyn Nagel, CEO of Watermark, shared an interesting story with me. Tough times had hit one of her previous companies. It had made some serious budget cuts for offsites. One of the managers really felt he needed to do an offsite. To economize and fit the event into the budget, he rented a large vacation house for the offsite. He figured the men on his team could all sleep there. He had one woman reporting to him. Rather than have her stay at the house with all the guys, he made reservations for her in a nearby hotel. While this move was well-intentioned, it made her the odd person out during the offsite. He was trying to be protective of her, but in reality, he ended up putting her at a huge disadvantage by isolating her from the rest of the team. Situations will always arise where you are not sure what's the right thing to do. In cases like these, always ask the woman, or even the team, "How can we make this work?"

Sometimes you will witness people doing the wrong thing. Wharton professor Adam Grant has made it a practice to intervene when he hears belittling or offensive remarks about women. Sometimes he will simply ask a quiet, gentle question: "What did you mean by that?" It's a nonconfrontational approach that often jars others into reflecting on what they've said and why, allowing them to come to their own realization about their behavior. Other times, Grant takes the offender aside to let them know that others are noticing their behavior and it is affecting their reputation.

We will not be able to fix this problem until a lot more people see it. The first step to a solution is to identify the problem, which is why this step is so important. Until people see it, there is nothing to fix. Once they see it, they can begin the journey toward understanding and change the dynamics.

7. Learn to cherish and leverage differences

So much power exists in understanding and being able to leverage differences. On the job, the difference in perspectives brings new understanding. In exploring our differences, we find the keys to innovation if we are all willing to listen and learn.

Model for Leveraging Differences

Now, I'd like to return to the framework we introduced in chapter one. We've expanded this framework as we have begun to understand how our differences affect the way we process, perceive, and what we value. The steps above will allow you to expand your secret decoder from the two-dimensional triangle we started with in the first chapter into a three-dimensional triangle-based pyramid.

Your decoder expands as you see how others process, perceive, and value things differently. As you gain more perspective, you are able to ask even more questions and continue to expand your knowledge and the knowledge of others. Figure 27 shows how the questions expand the triangle into a three-dimensional object. Each side of the three-dimensional triangle grows using the six steps listed above. The last step—being able to cherish and leverage our differences—is how you move from what was an impasse into a position of being able to leverage and cherish the differences productively in your workplace and in your life. As we understand each other and value the differences we all bring, we facilitate more innovation, market growth, and engagement.

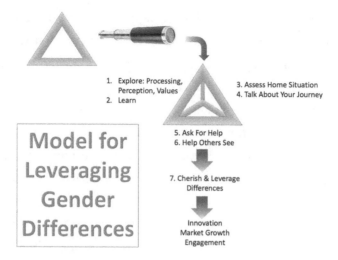

Figure 27: Model for Leveraging Gender Differences

COMPANY LEADERSHIP

You play a key role in the transformation of your workplace. As with many prizes in life, you "must be present" to win. By being present, I mean showing up, being engaged, and pulling all the levers you can. You set the stage for change and can drive it where it needs to go. This responsibility is not one you can delegate. This problem is not for HR to deal with. This issue is not for the head of diversity & inclusion to solve. It squarely rests on your shoulders, and that's where it needs to stay. Sure, other people can support you, but you own the vision of where you want to be—and you own the decisions to carve out the path to get there. Keep in mind that not making a decision *is* a decision. It is choosing not to care, which is a valid choice and the leadership team's prerogative. Too often, though, many leaders do not realize that by ignoring an issue, they are making a choice of inaction.

I had the opportunity to interview Art Kleiner, a strategy expert and the editor-in-chief of strategy+business, the management magazine published by PwC. I was drawn to him because of the book he co-authored with Jeffrey Schwarz, psychiatrist at UCLA School of Medicine and leading expert on neuroplasticity, and Josie Thomson, an award-winning executive coach and speaker, called *The Wise Advocate*.[122] The premise of the book is that there are two distinct patterns of mental activity and each of these patterns engages different circuits or paths in our brains. One, called the low ground, is associated with transactional leadership and short-term goals. The second pattern, high ground, is associated with long-term results, where we seek to break out of ordinary constraints and pursue more fundamental changes. In a subsequent article, the authors identified seven challenges that leaders face where they have the opportunity to choose either the transactional low ground or the more strategic high ground. Table 7 includes the seven challenges that must be overcome to be a strategic leader. Art, Josie, and Jeffrey

122 Kleiner, Art; Schwartz, Jeffrey; Thomson, Josie; *The Wise Advocate; The Inner Voice of Strategic Leadership*, Columbia Business School, 2019.

have even identified what you need to do to overcome these challenges.[123]

Challenge	How to Overcome this Challenge
Mastering impulse and emotion	Learn to cope with pressure without "acting out" in a reactive way
Thinking about what other people are thinking (mentalizing)	Paying explicit attention to others' thoughts and potential actions
Becoming habitually self-aware	"Mentalizing about yourself;" learning to recognize your own predispositions and capabilities
Integrating integrity with pragmatism	Balancing low and high ground mental activity; learning how to raise difficult issues in a safe and constructive way
Managing the side effects of success	Resisting the subtle cravings and temptations associated with authority and status
Expanding your aspirations	Giving vision and voice to broader and more significant goals; inspiring movement to achieve them
Building a legacy	Discerning what aspects of your true self will form your internal and external footprint (and are worth passing on to others)

Table 7: Seven Challenges to Overcome to Be a Strategic Leader

---

123 Schwartz, Jeffrey; Thomson, Josie, and Kleiner, Art; "The Seven Stages of Strategic Leadership; How to build the mental habits that enable you to make a living while making a better world," PwC strategy+business Magazine, July 26, 2019.

Five of these challenges really jumped out at me as the ones we need to drive the culture change to make the workplace not just hospitable, but great for all.

First, if we could learn to stop our knee-jerk reactions and start thinking about the implication of our reactions first, then wisely choosing how we respond, we would have gained some significant ground.

Trying to figure out what other people are thinking and what they might do is second. This is an excellent way to become more strategic and essentially drive your solutions to fit what other people need, I teach this skill in my strategic sales program and have found it to be an outstanding method of understanding your customers' needs in a way that fundamentally changes both the sales process and how you think about how clients make decisions.

Third, recognizing your own inclinations, becoming self-aware, allows you to install a decision point before you proceed. This is where you ask yourself, *Is this the way I want to proceed or am I picking a path based on past habits? Do I have other choices?* This directly relates to the first item under "Commit to Working on You" above, and to your newly expanding three-dimensional secret decoder.

How do you raise difficult issues? Often, the elephant in the room goes undiscussed, because it's just hard to bring these things up. So, fourth, be brave, and pick your timing, venue, and mode of discussion carefully. This is where leaders really need to stand up and say something. They may be the only people in the room who actually can initiate these conversations in a company.

Art shared a great story with me. In the early '80s, a Fortune 10 company started having management retreats. At this retreat, the company was celebrating the "customer comes first" movement and had all the trappings: balloons, banners, and cheering. Afterward, the top twenty-five men in the company went to dinner. One of them had a little too much to drink and got up to give a toast. He held up his glass and said: "The customer is not first. Joe our CEO is first, then Bob, the COO, is second. Third is John, our CFO...then the customer comes eighth." Everyone looked at Joe and waited. You could have heard a pin drop. This story was told to Art by the head of HR who was in the room, wondering what would happen next. Finally, Joe cracked a smile, and everyone cheered. The head of HR said it was the most honest communication he'd heard all year.

Art continued:

"The three biggest lies in corporate America are:

- The customer comes first.
- Employees are our greatest asset.
- We exist to offer returns to our shareholders."

The truth of the matter is that we are not fulfilling our corporate mission statements. Our purpose has morphed to filling the perceived needs of a core group of people who run the company. We are carrying around in our heads what we think these people need and acting on that information on a daily basis. We use this as a short-cut to respond to what we think Joe thinks. We act as if this were a proxy for the vision and mission statement. The problem with this approach is that we usually don't get what they want quite right and proceed to lead people a little off track. As this cascades downward in the organization, the "little off track" becomes bigger and bigger. If you've ever wondered why you have trouble reconciling what you've been asked to do in light of the company vision and mission, now you know how it goes awry.

We need to stop bowing to our "best guess" of what the leaders think and start having conversations to verify the direction ensuring that it aligns with the vision and mission of the company.

The last of the five: expanding your aspirations by giving vision and voice to broader and more significant goals and inspiring movement to achieve them are what we really need to drive the changes in our businesses. We need leaders to articulate where they want the company to be and how they plan to get there.

Rob Goffee and Gareth Jones, two gurus from the London School of Business, may have said it best in their book, *Why Should Anyone Work Here?*: [124]

---

124 Goffee, Rob and Jones, Gareth. *Why Should Anyone Work Here?: What it takes to create an authentic organization*, Harvard Business

"Authentic organizations of the future will foster environments where creativity and innovation are at a premium. Workplaces with these qualities look for an unusual kind of diversity, hiring people for differences that are more than skin deep," they write. "Differences in thought processes, frames of reference and skills among other things. These companies surround themselves with people whose differences in perspectives, habits of mind and core assumptions would challenge them and push them in new directions."

As you can see, this is really a strategic imperative. Some might hazard to say, "Yes, it's a strategic imperative, but it has no urgency." I beg to differ. Ask the former employees of Nokia, Polaroid, Blockbuster, or Borders if they'd wished their leadership teams had put some urgency on defining their company culture in a way that might have kept them afloat. These companies did not move fast enough, nor did they stay in tune with their customers' needs. What's worse is at least one of them, Polaroid, had the keys to unleash innovation. One of their engineers came to them early on and showed them what they could do with digital pictures. Their executives, realizing that this new technology could undermine their entire business model, politely asked the engineer to not continue with his development and not talk

---

Review Press, 2015.

about his work with others. Talk about burying your head in the sand! They had access to new technology they could have owned and chose to throw the proverbial keys into the gutter. And then the contents of the gutter rose up and basically consumed their company.

To create a vision for your organization, you need to consider six broad imperatives, according to the authors of *Why Should Anyone Work Here?* As you read these imperatives and their defining characteristics, ask yourself: how would the people in your organization, including the women, react to these imperatives? How would the people in your organization rank your company against these yardsticks?

- Difference: I want to work in a place where I can be myself, where I can express the ways in which I am different and how I see things differently.
- Radical Honesty: I want to know what's really going on.
- Extra Value: I want to work in an organization that magnifies my strengths and adds extra value for me and my personal development.
- Authenticity: I want to work in an organization I'm proud of, one that truly stands for something.
- Meaning: I want my day-to-day work to be meaningful.
- Simple Rules: I do not want to be hindered by stupid rules or rules that apply to some people but not others.

These six imperative clusters are simple and clear. How are you going to enact them in your company?

UNDERSTAND WHAT PEOPLE NEED

When we first started working thousands of years ago, everyone was doing what they needed to do to survive. We became more specialized, honing our skills in certain areas, getting paid for that work, and using our earnings to meet our other needs. The dairy farmer used his earnings to buy wood to build a new barn and by doing so supported the lumberjack.

As the Industrial Age matured, handcrafted products gave way to production lines because they offered efficiency to the production process. More cars and a host of other products could be produced with fewer people. New roles emerged associated with production lines while less manual labor was needed. At the time, no one seemed to put much thought into how the production line workers felt about turning the same screw hundreds of times per day. Job satisfaction was not much of a concern. The investment by the company had been in establishing the production line. The people who worked the line were thought of more like commodities. The goal was to boost production.

As we fast forward to today's knowledge workers, you see a very different dynamic. We now hire people for their minds and what they can do with them. We need creative, imaginative people who can apply what they know to the problems of today to create the products and solutions of tomorrow.

"The significant problems we face cannot be solved at the same level of thinking we were at when we created them," as Albert Einstein said.

One of the most important considerations is what knowledge workers need in order to thrive.

After researching the topic and drawing from several well-known experts, I have compiled a short list of what you need to attract and retain this group of people shown in Table 8. You will notice that this list is focused on intangibles. These are the five key ingredients for satisfying work. If you offer these, they will come, stay, and be engaged.

Key Ingredient	Description
Autonomy	The ability to guide some portion of one's own work
Complexity	Knowledge workers need intellectual challenge in their jobs. Give them problems to solve, that's how they learn
Meaning/ Purpose	Finding meaning and purpose in one's work allows people to live their passion
Lifelong Learners	Knowledge workers are fed by learning, help keep them primed
Authenticity	I want to work in a place where I can be myself, and people appreciate me for the differences I bring

Table 8: Five Key Ingredients for Satisfying Work

TEAMS ALSO HAVE NEEDS

Several years ago, Google set out to determine what makes a perfect team, calling it Project Aristotle. [125]Google not only studied but also measured nearly every aspect of employees' behavior. The researchers interviewed hundreds of employees and studied 180 teams within Google to try and discover the secret ingredient. They looked at personality types, background, education, you name it.

For years, Google had been known to only hire the best and brightest. Some on the team believed that was the key to great teamwork. Only hire the best and brightest—it was their short-cut, their secret decoder.

Imagine Google's surprise when the data was compiled. The first stunning conclusion was the researchers could find no patterns based on "who" the team members were—personality type, skills, hobbies, education, even whether the team members hung out together outside of work.

In frustration, they decided to dig deeper and look at the group "norms" or "unwritten rules" of engagement. You know, things like: do people talk over others at meetings or do they take turns talking?

What they found to be important was not who the team members were, but how the team members together interact, structure their work, and view their contributions. The key secret ingredient they discovered was psychological safety,

---

125 Duhigg, Charles; "What Google Learned from Its Quest to Build the Perfect Team," The New York Times Magazine, Feb 25, 2016.

"a sense of confidence that the team will not embarrass, reject or punish someone for speaking up," according to Harvard Business School professor Amy Edmondson.

The five key dynamics for successful teams at Google were:

1. **Psychological safety:** Can we take risks on this team without feeling insecure or embarrassed?
2. **Dependability:** Can we count on each other to do high-quality work on time?
3. **Structure & clarity:** Are goals, roles, and execution plans on our team clear?
4. **Meaning of work:** Are we working on something that is personally important for each of us?
5. **Impact of work:** Do we fundamentally believe that the work we're doing matters?

The three years of intense effort at Google had uncovered what good managers have always known: the best teams listen to each other and show sensitivity to others' feeling and needs.

Google then proceeded to try and discover how you go about creating psychological safety. That was a much harder nut to crack and, in the process, Google had to talk about the findings within the company. One manager, Matt, who had just taken over a new team, heard about their findings and asked his new team to take some of the surveys to see where he was starting from with his team.

He was surprised to see his team was not doing so well. So, he scheduled an offsite where the team could talk about their survey results. Matt opened the meeting by asking people to share something deeply personal about themselves. He went first and told the group that he had stage-four cancer. Others shared their own stories: other health issues, relationships gone awry, and much more.

Then, when it came time to discuss the survey results, the conversation was much easier. The emotional window had already flown open, and people were more comfortable talking about things that scared them. They were also equally open to discussing their hopes and dreams.

Matt was the leader of that team, and the leader plays a critical role for the team.

The behaviors that create psychological safety—conversational turn-taking and empathy—are part of the same unwritten rules we often turn to, as individuals, when we need to establish a bond. And those human bonds matter as much at work as anywhere else; in fact, they sometimes matter more.

Project Aristotle has taught the people within Google that no one wants to put on a "work face" when they get to the office. No one wants to leave part of their personality and inner life at home. But to be fully present at work, to feel "psychologically safe," we must know that we can be free enough, sometimes, to share what scares us without fear of recrimination. We must be able to talk about what is messy or sad, to have hard conversations with colleagues who are driving us crazy. We can't be focused just on efficiency. Rather, when we start the morning by collaborating with a team of engineers and then send emails to our marketing colleagues and then jump on a conference call, we want to know that those people really hear us. We want to know that work is more than just labor.

"Just having data that proves to people that these things are worth paying attention to sometimes is the most important step in getting them to actually pay attention," advises Julia Rozovsky, lead researcher at Yale working on Google teams. "Don't underestimate the power of giving people a common platform and operating language."

I believe we can all apply what Google has learned about successful teams to our companies. We must be careful that, as we look at gender differences and differences in people in general, we do not inadvertently undermine our own efforts based on how we process information or work, how we perceive the world, or what we place value on.

DIFFERENCES ARE KEY

Throughout this book, we have examined a variety of differences that exist between the genders and in people in general. There are many more that were not discussed here, and I expect many more will come as science continues to offer us more in-depth explanations of human behavior. Share this information and open up dialogue in your workplace on these topics. Add into your culture the ability to cele-brate differences.

I think that Liz Wiseman, in her book, *Multipliers*, gave the best definition of culture and what critical bits are needed to make it work: [126]

> From an anthropological perspective, culture is "the beliefs, customs, arts, etc, of a particular society, group, place, or time." From the business perspective, culture is "a way of thinking, behaving, or working that exists in a place or organization."

> Strong cultures typically exhibit the following traits:
> - Common language: words and phrases that hold a common meaning within a community based on opinions, principles, and values.
> - Learned behaviors: a set of learned responses to stimuli.
> - Shared beliefs: the acceptance of something that is true.
> - Heroes and legends: people who are admired or ide-alized for their qualities, behavior, and/or achieve-ments and the stories told about their heroic actions.
> - Rituals and norms: consistent behavior regularly fol-lowed by an individual or a group.

126 Wiseman, Liz. *Multipliers: How the Leaders Make Everyone Smarter.* *HarperBusiness*, 2017.

Use these traits to help incorporate the valuing of differences in your culture. Develop a common language that works for you and is based on your culture, learning, and industry. Ensure that people become comfortable talking about differences, what those mean, and how they've benefited.

Learned behaviors are just that: learned. Jon Katzenbach, author of *The Critical Few*, summarized the important bits about changing behaviors from the expert on *The Power of Habit*, Charles Duhigg:

> "In other words, if you want to change the way people think, you don't start with or rely primarily on rational argument," Katzenbach explains. "You change what they do, even if it doesn't come naturally to them at first. Over time, as the new behavior becomes a pattern, they will likely change how they feel about doing it. They will see rewards or results of some kind, and those generate positive emotions; those emotions then become associated with the action, encouraging it to be repeated."

So you get them to change their behavior, and then they will be able to wrap their heads around the desired behaviors. This activity, if done right, will lead to the shared beliefs.

Seek out the heroes and legends in your organization and share them. Memorialize the stories you want to hear repeated throughout the organization. While you're at it, create rituals and norms that you want everyone to follow.

GET YOUR BUSINESS LEADERS ENGAGED

Under the guise of getting male business leaders engaged, I would suggest that having your male leaders not just attend but also participate in women's organizations and conferences will accelerate their growth tremendously. Send a few of your leaders to several of these conferences. One of the ways I have found to enrich people's understanding is to have them prepare a presentation or discussion of the things they learned to share with the rest of the team upon their return from an event. When people know going in that they will have to do so, I find that they listen differently, recognizing that they will need to be able to explain discussions and topics to others.

To help your leaders with this task, I wanted to pass on some very helpful recommendations from David Smith and Brad Johnson, co-authors of *Athena Rising*.[127] The information in the callout below is a brief mindset tutorial from David and Brad to set your executives up for success.

---

127 Johnson, Brad W and Smith, David. *Athena Rising: How and Why Men Should Mentor Women*. Routledge, 2018.

HOW MEN CAN BE BETTER ALLIES

Thoughtfully Shared by: David Smith & W. Brad Johnson

Here are some tangible recommendations for men who are invited to participate in women's conferences or other initiatives as allies for gender equality in the workplace. These are best practices for men who want to be better collaborators with women.

First, just listen! Consultant Chuck Shelton reminds men that listening to women's voices in a way that inspires trust and respect is a fundamental relationship promise you must make, and then keep, with women who invite you to participate around equity. Generous, world-class listening requires focus, sincerity, empathy, refusal to interrupt, and genuine valuing of both her experience and her willingness to share it with you.

Respect the space. Women's conferences and employee resource groups (ERGs) are often one outgrowth of experiences of exclusion, marginalization, and discrimination. Many of these experiences are painful. Large events and local resource groups have afforded women a powerful platform for sharing experiences, providing support, and strategizing equity initiatives. Tread respectfully into these spaces and, before you utter a word, revisit the recommendation above.

Remember, it's not about you. Ask women how you can amplify, not replace or usurp, existing gender parity efforts. A large dose of gender humility will help here. Decades of research on prosocial (helpful) behavior reveals a stark gender difference in how it is expressed. While women often express helpfulness communally and relationally, men show helpful intentions through action-oriented behaviors. Sometimes, we need to rein this impulse in. Refrain from taking center stage, speaking for women, or mansplaining how women should approach gender equity efforts.

Get comfortable being uncomfortable. Developing psychological standing requires a commitment to learning and advocating for gender equity. Learning about the professional challenges of women may produce feelings of self-shame or self-blame that cause anxiety. The solution is more interaction and learning, not less.

Engage in supportive partnerships with women. The best cross-gender ally relationships are reciprocal and mutually growth-enhancing. Share your social capital (influence, information, knowledge, and organizational resources) with women's groups but ask them—don't assume—how you can best support their efforts.

Remember the two parts to allyship. Keep in mind that committing to express as little sexism as possible in your interactions with women is the easy part of allyship. The hard part requires you to take informed action. Use your experience in women's events and initiatives to learn how you can best become a public ally for social justice around gender. When the time comes, this may require you to upset the status quo.

SET GOALS

The best way to get organizational alignment is to set some goals and then hold your teams accountable. We are all familiar with this process, and it works. Get the organization involved with the goal-setting. It's part of the dialogue you want to instigate, and the conversations need to happen to achieve alignment or discover early on that your goals need to be adjusted.

PROFESSIONAL ORGANIZATIONS

Many women's organizations have sprung up over the last thirty years to support women. While I love these organizations, I am not sure if they aren't in some ways perpetuating the problem. Many of these organizations focus on "fixing" women, so that they can compete in the male world of business. When we do this, we are setting women up for failure. What we are telling them is "do these things and you'll be successful." Honestly, we've been trying this approach for thirty years and it hasn't worked. I hardly expect it to become a magic elixir now. What we really need to do is change the unwritten rules of business and get people to open up their conversations to include the emotional impact they feel at work.

For these organizations:

- Expand your educational programs to include men and women together (aim for 50/50 participation).

- Focus on understanding and leveraging our differences.
- Offer tools and training that help people discuss their emotions and how their lives and work are going.
- Set a goal to share success stories (there are already plenty of horror stories out there): people need to see that improvements are being made and understand who the game-changers are and that they are making a difference. My You Can't Fix What You Can't See podcast has a series called 'Secrets of Success'. I will be interviewing companies with success stories to tell so we can amplify our collective learning. Find out more on the website: www.YouCantFixWhatYouCantSee.com.
- Get male business leaders engaged.

***

Today, I can picture a different working environment for our kids. A place where people are respected for the differences that they bring into the workplace. A place where differences in how we process information, how we perceive the world, and what we value are respected. A place where innovation, market growth, and engagement thrive based on our ability to leverage and capitalize on our differences.

It's a place we still need to create, so let's get started. After all, You Can't Fix What You Can't See!

ACKNOWLEDGMENTS

In creating this book, I had a unique opportunity to interview many different people. Each conversation taught me something, each conversation was a chance to test my model to see if it held true. All these conversations allowed me to move one step closer to making this book a reality. My journey has been tremendous and many people have helped shape this book. Their time and effort will make it easier for the people who read this book to decide they too have had enough. And to inspire them to take the initiative to reshape the business world so it is one where our children and the generations that follow them can truly thrive. Here are the many people who I interviewed and helped shape this book:

Ray Arata – Founder of Better Man Conference, Keynote speaker, Co-Founder Inclusionary Leadership Group

Avi Ben-Zeev – Psychology Professor and Diversity, Equity & Inclusion Speaker & Researcher

Ruth Chandler Cook – Founder & CEO HireHer

Crystal Davis – CEO & Principal Lean Practitioner, DisrupTHER Coach

Lori Eberly – Executive Coach, Keynote Speaker, Co-Author of *Fuckery*

Tasha Eurich – Author of *Insight: The Surprising Truth about How Others See Us, How We See Ourselves, and Why the Answers Matter More than We Think*, Organizational Psychologist, Keynote Speaker

Davida Ewan – Senior Engineer, Pacific Biosciences

Bill Fitzsimmons – Retired EVP of Regulatory Affairs, Clinical and Research Quality Assurance at Japan-based Pharmaceutical Company Astellas

Jeffrey Tobias Halter – Gender Strategist, Founder YWomen, Author of *WHY Women: The Leadership Imperative to Advancing Women and Engaging Men*

Wendy Hanson – Co-Founder & COO at BetterManager

Sarah Hedges – 5th Grade Teacher & PhD Physicist

Ed Hoffman – Founder Knowledge Strategies, LLC; Senior Lecturer on Information & Knowledge Strategy, Columbia University, former Chief Knowledge Officer of NASA

Steve Kerr – Author, Speaker, Consultant

Christine King – Operations Director at Nucleation Capital

Art Kliener – Editor-in-Chief, PwC Global and Strategy + Business, co-Author *The Wise Advocate: The Inner Voice of Strategic Leadership*

Joanne Lipman – Author of *That's What She Said: What Men Need to Know (And Women Need to Tell Them) About Working Together* and CNBC Contributor, former Editor in Chief of USA Today

Nilofer Merchant – Speaker and Author of *The Power of Onlyness: Make Your Wild Ideas Mighty Enough to Dent the World*

Henry Miller – Speaker with Power Passion, and Purpose

Marilyn Nagel – Chief Learning Officer of SAMI game, CEO of Watermark, and former Chief Diversity Officer Cisco

Julius Pryor III – Chair of the Board of Directors for Healthcare Innovation

Jay Pryor – Executive Advisor, Keynote Speaker, Founder Jay Pryor Consulting, LLC

Kim Scott – Author of *Radical Candor: Be a Kickass Boss without Losing Your Humanity*

Declan Shalvey – Executive Advisor and Board Member

David Smith – PhD Associate Professor of Sociology at Naval War College & Co-Author of *Athena Rising*

Myra Strober – Professor Emerita, Stanford University, author of *Sharing the Work: What my Family and Career Taught me about Breaking Through (and Holding the Door Open for Others)*

Sally Thorton – CEO & Founder of Forshay and WorkLab-Accelerator, Speaker

Kathryn Ullrich – Head of US Diversity Practice at Ogers Berndtson

Liz Wiseman – Author of *Multipliers: How the Best Leaders Make Everyone Smarter*

There are also others who agreed to be my Advanced Readers who provided invaluable feedback on early versions of the manuscript. I applaud these brave souls as early manuscripts prior to professional editing are always going to be a challenge. Your perspectives and feedback have shaped this book tremendously and everyone who reads it appreciates the extra effort you put forth:

Dale Tibbils	**Scott Pease**
Christine King	**Kim McAskill**
PT Tran	**Lisa Stapleton**

It takes a village to publish a book and I had a full court press along the publication journey. I want to give a special heap of thanks to:

Eric Koester – Who is Creating Creators

Brian Bies – Publishing Guru Extraordinaire of New Degree Press

Lauryn Younge – For asking me that simple question, "Do you want to Write a Book?"

Bailee Tracy – My Awesome Marketing editor

Ashley Goodnow - My Fantastic Developmental Editor

Catriona Kendall – My Master Copy Editor

ChandaElaine Spurlock – Goddess of Editors

Stefan Mancevski – My Book Cover Designer

Amanda Brown – Goddess of Copy Editors

Finally, this book would not have been possible without my tribe of supporters who put their faith out on a limb and believed enough in me to know I should be an author. Extra-Special thanks to Super Fans in **Bold**:

Paul Arnao	Lawrence Chi
Tom Augello	Lana Chou
Yixiu Bagley	Jim Corcoran
Bonita Banducci	David Cornwell
John Bates	Jennifer Correa
Maryann Baumgarten	Katherine Davidson
Avi Ben-Zeev	Margy Day
Barbara Berman	Frank Del Fiugo
Lisa Bohorquez	**Sandra A Delvin**
Betty Branlund	Tim Duffey
Beverly Cairel	Jeff Duran
Jorge J Perez Castedo	Suzi Edwards -Alexander
Amber Lee Caton	Christina Enneking
Laura Kathleen Chandler	Darrell Esau

Ruby M Escalada

Carolyn Evanoff

Marcus Fischer

Raul Flores

Dawn Flores

William J Franklin

Elisha Gargiulo

Kim Gaxiola

Erika George

Estee Solomon Gray

Bettyanne Green

Kevin Greteman

Lisa Griswold

Claudio Guffanti

Phyllis Hecht

Sarah J Hedges

Mark Richard Heinold

Anita Herrmann

Jim Hicks

Gabrielle Hildebrand

Katherine Ivey

Donald Janecek

Janet Janssen

Sarah Johnson

Madison Jones

Christine King

Rachel Kirkley

Eric Koester

G. Vijay Kumar

Lisa Kunze

Judy Kusa

Loria Kutch

Hilda Lafebre

Virginia Larsen

Douglas Larson

Julie & Tim Leong

Anna Leskova

Elaine Lung

Kim MacAskill

Ben MacAskill

Pat Marriott

Natalie Martin-Smith

Megan Mayer

Renee H McCain

Eddie McMorrow

Lorrie McPheeters

Dane Mechlin

Gabriel Michael

Marc Miller

Suzie Moore

Jodi Muirhead

Hung Viet Nguyen

John and Mary Ellen Nowel

Eunhee Oh

Dan Pappone

Ana Paz-Rangel

Josephine Phua

Joy Pogalies

DeLisa Pournaras

Carlos Puig

Amber Ramey

David Rodeck

Wanda I. Roman

Joel Ruiz

Allie Scott

Judi Seip

Joie Seldon

Declan Shalvey

Carolyn Shockley

Lisa K Stapleton

Kurt Joseph Stuve

Gill Thacker

Dale Tibbils

PT Tran

Josine Verhagen

Hugh Walker

Brendon Wilson

Denise Woernle

David Wu

Miki Yoshida

Lauryn F. Younge

Jody Zetterquist